BAND OF STRANGERS

JAMES K. CULLEN

Dedication

This book is dedicated to my own dear Carol for the many hours of typing and re-typing on our computer. She wrestled with my scribbles and a Word program that had a mind of its own. In addition, she sweetly frowned at my bad grammar and syntax and inserted big question marks at questionable phrases. Without her there would be no book.

CONTENTS

Part II

ACKNOWLEDGEMENTS

The great writer, Ernie Pyle, said that it is true that the majority of front-line infantrymen did not have the vaguest idea where they were during the fighting, nor did they really care—survival was the important thing! As a result, I had to do a lot of research in the National Archives and military history books to find out where I was in France, Belgium and Germany during 1944 and 1945.

Stephen Ambrose and others have pictured us, the "dogfaces", as a closely-knit group of men going arm-in-arm into the Battle. They call us, as Shakespeare wrote, "A Band of Brothers." That's not what I experienced during the fighting in the European Theatre of Operations, and in the book, you will see why I call this a "Band of Strangers."

Over the years since 1945 I have met in person or through e-mail, sons and daughters and grandchildren who were desperate to know where their parents and grandparents were in the War. They wanted to know where they fought, and how they died. As a result, I decided, after talking it over with my wife, Carol, to write about the War as I saw it and as I remember it.

These pages are for Cathie and Jim, and Allegra and VJ. They didn't know me back then. They're also for the rest of my family who shared in the experience of living through World War II.

It is not easy to put on paper memories from more than sixty years ago. In an effort to jog my memories, I turned to the National Archives II in College Park, MD and the Military History Institute at Carlisle Barracks, PA. Officials at both places were friendly and helpful, and gave invaluable assistance by pointing out the books that told the story of the 3rd Armored Division, books that I did not know existed.

Sincere thanks to Mark McFadden, Peter Hefferan, Lark Berhman, and all the people at Picatinny Arsenal, N.J. who made our Battle of the Bulge Group welcome over the years. They briefed us on today's army and let us find out how heavy an M-1 and B.A.R. have grown over the years.

I must also thank my re-enactor friends, Steve Borts, Chuck Anderson, Tom Allen and the rest of the group, who welcomed me on a visit to the west coast. They inspired me, through their enthusiasm and questions, to think deeply about the 3rd Armored Division and to write about my experiences in WWII.

My good friends in Belgium, Henri Rogister and Anne Marie Noel-Simon and her husband, Karl Heinz, aided me in clearing up the mystery of where my company fought in Belgium. Mr. Rogister gave me detailed, day-to-day action reports of our fighting, and Anne Marie helped me with the identity of the "civilian" who was killed in Eupen.

We have corresponded many times over the years since our first contact, and thankfully I have been able to get information for them from the Archives for their work in CRIBA (Center of Research and Information on the Battle of the Bulge).

Thanks also to my own Cathie, Jim and Kat for reading the rough copies of these pages. They gave me good advice and some valuable corrections. Allegra and VJ, my dear grandchildren, offered encouragement while I was writing down my memories and gave me another reason to do so. They will see a side of their grandfather they never knew or thought he ever was – a young man.

I want to thank my daughter-in-law, Kat, for the many hours spent digitizing my manuscript. To my editor, Helen Nazzaro at One More Time Editing, my cover artist, James Price of James Price Designs, and Nazzaro & Price Publishing, thank you for your help and expertise in bringing my story to life for generations to come.

FOREWORD

Imagine being a young soldier, newly assigned to an unfamiliar unit, and expected to lead an infantry squad into combat on terrain that was never anticipated, and for which there was no doctrine, training, or even suggestions on how to proceed.

This is the situation that confronted Staff Sergeant Jim Cullen in July 1944. His experience was not that of a "band of brothers" who had known each other all the way through training; but a "band of strangers" who were thrown together piecemeal and expected to complete the mission during some of the fiercest fighting of the war.

The hedgerows of Normandy were where Jim Cullen and others got their first taste of combat, and the infantry bore the brunt of the fighting - terrible day after terrible day. They learned lessons paid for in blood, adapted, and overcame the natural obstacles of the hedgerows, and defeated the German defenders.

Walking the hedgerows almost 70 years later, I was in awe of what these men accomplished. The hedgerows are nearly perfect defensive obstacles, blocking sight and sound, and funneling attackers into narrow lanes with no room to maneuver except straight up the road. Yet, our soldiers emerged victorious.

As a young soldier defending the Fulda Gap with the 3rd Armored Division in 1973, I often thought of the American soldiers that persevered during the Battle of the Bulge. European winters can be harsh and unforgiving. The American soldiers of World War II faced the combined hardships of a brutal winter and a determined enemy. Again, they emerged victorious.

Having a small taste of the hardships faced by our soldiers in World War II, I gained a new appreciation, more like a reverence, for their accomplishments.

As I tell Jim Cullen every year when I send him a note

on V-E day: "Thank you for saving the world."

This story should bring a new appreciation of the difficulties faced by the American soldier in Europe, plus some anecdotes, both humorous and poignant.

Thank you for sharing this story.

Steven K. Borts

First Sergeant - 3rd Armored Div. Retired

U.S. Army

.

BAND OF STRANGERS

PROLOGUE

James K. Cullen II

Third Generation

When I was growing up in the 1960s and 1970s, being the son of a World War II veteran was not normal. Most of the kids my age had fathers who had never served in the military, being either too young for WWII or too old for Vietnam. My father's life had been delayed a bit due to his time in the war and the injuries he received, so he didn't have children until later than most men of his generation. He was already 40 years old when I was born. He jokingly signed his notes "D.O.D", for "Dear Old Dad". I usually called him "Pop".

D.O.D. was the second generation of our family who had seen combat in a world war. My grandfather Martin had been wounded in combat in World War I during his time with the Argyll and Sutherland Highlanders, a Scottish infantry unit. My grandfather and my dad, despite being wounded in battle, each came home and put those horrors behind them and stoically got to work learning their trades and raising their families.

Although during my childhood my dad never dwelled on the battles that he or his father had fought, some reminders were always present. As a young boy I remember my grandmother casually hand-knitting me a wool balaclava "helmet liner" to keep my ears warm in the winter, and her mentioning "making them for the boys" during World War I. For my Boy Scout camping trips, my dad dug around in the basement and came up with a G.I.-issued World War II olive drab mess kit and canteen. On his bookshelves I found a library ranging from Bill Mauldin "Up Front" cartoon books to detailed analyses of land and sea battles in the European and Pacific theaters, and many books and photo collections about the 3rd Armored Division. In the far back of a closet in the spare bedroom was Pop's old olive drab Army jacket, with rows of ribbons and the 3rd Armored Division "Spearhead" patch on the sleeve. I would try it on from time to time (my dad probably doesn't know that).

My mother would remind us to speak loudly because of D.O.D.'s "artillery lag" (even as a young man, he had significant hearing loss in both ears from the gunfire and explosions he had been exposed to).

My father's physical scars were always there for us to see, as a constant reminder of what he had been through. My mom would quietly caution us to keep an eye out and let her or Pop know if he hurt himself, because he wouldn't know it if it happened. He had no sensation in the lower half of his leg, and couldn't feel anything from the knee down. I remember him cutting his foot badly on a sharp object while walking barefoot on the beach, leaving bloody footprints in the sand until one of us caught up and told him he was injured.

Although he certainly qualified for special parking privileges and handicapped license plates, he refused to get them (still, to this day) because he felt there was always someone who needed it more than him.

When you grow up in that environment, it makes you think about what your father has been through, and why he went through it. I grew up with a lot of curiosity about World War II and the men like my father who served in that war, and with great admiration for the sense of duty, service to country, and personal sacrifice displayed by them.

Growing up in the Woodstock era as the son of a World War II veteran meant that some of the words, phrases, and images of my childhood had very different meanings to me than to my peers. When other kids said "Mustang", I thought about the P-51 fighter plane and not the car from Ford. When they said "Corvette", I thought of a small fighting ship and not the Chevrolet sports car. I found it strange that TV shows like "Hogan's Heroes" made the German military look stupid, clumsy, and incompetent, when I knew they were smart, capable, and very dangerous. It disturbed me when I saw LIFE Magazine articles or TV news clips of American soldiers being jeered and spit on by protestors as they returned from Vietnam, as I had always viewed the American military as being good, honorable, and worthy of respect.

As a kid, I enjoyed making plastic models of ships and airplanes, occasionally an Army tank. Pop would join me. Sometimes we'd work on the same model together, and sometimes we'd work on separate projects at the same table. One time he made a model of a green "half-track" vehicle, essentially an armored truck with tank-style treads and a heavy machine gun mounted on top. The large block numbers on the side read "E-12", and in smaller white letters, "ELEANOR". He explained to me that "Eleanor" had been the armored vehicle that was assigned to him in World War II, when he was in charge of a team of soldiers. He told me a few stories about his travels with Eleanor, and how a group of strangers gathered from all over the country were thrown together to fight a very dangerous and evil enemy. I of course wanted to learn more, and know why this happened. By that point in my life I had learned about the Holocaust and the atrocities carried out by the Nazi regime, and I wanted to understand why and how people do such horrific and unspeakable things to other human beings. Pop explained that throughout history there have been bad people who would take advantage of others and conquer them and do terrible things to them, unless good people rose up to stop them. I realized that my dad and his men had been the "good people".

I always knew my father was different in the sense he was older than other kids' dads, but he was also very different in his bearing, character, and morals. Although he was an immigrant to the United States, he was fiercely patriotic and did not take for granted the good life in this country. When World War II broke out in Europe and it became clear this conflict was spreading around the globe, he attempted to volunteer for the U.S. Army Air Corps. Turned down because he was not a citizen, he went to Canada to try to join the Royal Air Force to fight the Germans. Called back to the USA by a telegram when his father was struck by a car in New Jersey, he was helping support his family when he was finally drafted by the U.S. Army.

D.O.D. was a quiet role model to me and to my sister Cathie, in the way he loved, respected, and looked out for our mother Carol. As a boy, he taught me to protect my sister, to protect others who could not protect themselves, and to always stand up to bullies. After my mother would spend time teaching me to "talk things out" and attempt to negotiate with bullies, my father would take me aside and say "some people don't understand words; they can only understand one thing. If someone crosses the line and hits you, you have to hit them back, *hard*. They will certainly understand that."

When I was a rebellious teenager, Dad patiently stuck with me through some tough life lessons learned from hanging out with the wrong crowd (I found myself sitting in the back seat of a police car years prior to when I was hired to drive one). He reminded me to live honorably and do the right thing even if no one else was watching, to live a life that my mother and grandmother would be proud of, and to treat others the way you would want them to treat you. He also taught me that having responsibility for the safety and well-being of others is one of the most important and sacred duties a man can have.

Years later, as I grew up and moved into positions as a police supervisor and then as a military NCO, I drew upon Dad's lessons and his example when I was placed in charge of police squads and military units. I realized the importance of the responsibility placed upon me to take care of my people and to make sure they came home safely.

During those model-building days of my childhood, my Pop spent a lot of time studying old pictures to make sure his E-12 ELEANOR model was done accurately. He even melted a large hole through the armor near the gun ring on top to recreate the damage from a German shell punching a hole through the real "Eleanor" during one battle where my dad was injured and other men died. This of course sparked conversation about the young men assigned to "Eleanor", several of whom never came home. At one point D.O.D. mentioned climbing up the side of the halftrack after it was hit, to try to rescue the men inside. I realized that he was putting the well-being and safety of his men first, and their welfare ahead of himself; despite the halftrack being under fire by a German tank, instead of running <u>away</u> from the danger he was running TOWARD his men to try to help them. The concept of "service to others above self" sunk in, and inspired me as I continued on to careers in law enforcement, emergency medical services, and the military. Based upon my father's example, I always tried to take care of my people and put the men and women I worked with first.

When the terrorist attacks of September 11, 2001 happened, by coincidence I had just graduated from Officer Candidates' School and it was my very first day as a commissioned military officer. Unable to reach my command by telephone, I strapped my police department gun belt over my military uniform and headed toward New York City. I called every other Reservist I knew in New Jersey as I drove, telling them to meet me at a rendezvous point in New York Harbor. Cell phone service was quickly becoming overwhelmed. As I crossed onto the New Jersey Turnpike extension and drove toward the collapsed towers of the World Trade Center, I called my parents before the static took over and spoke to my dad briefly. "I don't know what I'm heading into right now or what I'm going to do there, but for the first time in my life I think I have just the slightest feeling of what you must have felt like during the war." Dad wished me luck, and I knew he understood what I was feeling.

Only a few minutes later, I found myself in charge of a group of strangers who were looking to me for guidance and leadership in the face of something horrific and overwhelming. I asked myself, "What would D.O.D. do in this situation?" Remembering my dad's lifelong lessons and his own daily demonstrations of personal strength and courage in the face of adversity carried me through the hours and weeks that followed.

Many other groups of strangers found themselves thrown together that day to try to do the right thing. Whether in New York City, at the Pentagon, or in the skies over Pennsylvania, good people – many who had never met before – banded together and rose up to fight evil.

The events of 9/11 changed the arc of my life, and I spent the next several years serving more often as a military officer than a police officer. Eight years later when I was training to deploy to Iraq and Afghanistan, I brought all of my deployment gear to my parents' house for them to see how technology had changed. My dad and I talked about what I might be heading into, and how I might be tested by it...

CHAPTER ONE

The More Things Change
James K. Cullen I

Someone once said that the more things change, the more they stay the same. This is especially true in warfare. The soldiers in Iraq and Afghanistan are super-equipped compared to our 1944 gear. I've lifted one of their body armor vests, and the thing weighed more than thirty-five pounds. Knee pads, elbow pads, Camelbacks of water, and extra ammo magazines are all hung onto the poor GI's back, and this is in combat, not on a march. WWII soldiers went in with as little as possible, particularly in hot weather. On a pair of suspenders, we hung a cartridge belt or pistol belt that carried a canteen of water and a medical pouch. Sometimes we folded a raincoat on the back of the belt. A light musette bag with K rations in it was slung over our shoulder if we were going to be away from the half-track for a while. All our gear did not approach thirty-five pounds—not even near that.

Weapons are different in weight, and the new GI has the advantage in this. Our M-1 weighed 9.8 pounds. The new M-16 weighs 7.6 pounds, the M-4 is 6.5 pounds, but they can throw a lot more lead faster than we ever could.

What has stayed the same are the faces of the soldiers. They look just like we did in 1943, 1944, and 1945. Their eyes have that same tired, wary look we had. Our faces were dirty with beards, now these desert soldiers are usually clean-shaven, but very dusty.

Today's soldiers have been doing city fighting—the most dangerous kind, just as thousands of us did in Europe during the 1940s. It takes a lot of guts to push at a door or look through a window and not know what is going to happen next. In doing that, you remember what happened two days ago when the squad leader opened a door and the house exploded in his face.

I feel for these men who are in close combat, but I feel most sorry for the GIs caught by an IED (improvised explosive device) alongside a road. These two hundred fifty and five-hundred-pound bombs are killers, and there is no way to hit back immediately at the enemy. Eventually these bombers are rooted out, but it is always after the fact as they don't stick around to fight.

I also suppose there is a difference in another aspect of the fighting against terrorists. We had a bit of respect for the German soldier who faced us, even the SS. We were fighting a uniformed, trained army who usually acted in a "normal" manner and usually followed the rules of engagement. This new enemy is not in our war manuals and follows no rules. He wraps a bomb around himself and blows himself away; or straps a bomb to a woman or child and sends them to their deaths. What a way to fight a war!

We were ordinary American GIs, unexpectedly banded together.

In 2001, another band of strangers fought a common enemy. They were passengers in an airplane—United Airlines Flight 93—the hijacked aircraft that crashed into a field in Pennsylvania. Those passengers didn't even know each other's names, but under pressure they had the will to do the job that they knew they had to do—even if it killed them.

Those men on that plane, strangers to each other—and we soldiers on the ground, strangers also—were united with common beliefs, resolves and hopes. Infantrymen, when pinned down by enemy fire, could lie there in a field and wait to be killed, or we could get on our feet, hold tight to our rifle and go toward the enemy. This same resolve to fight no doubt drove the civilians on Flight 93.

CHAPTER TWO
Replacements

I stepped onto Omaha Beach, Normandy, and didn't get my feet wet.

It was the first week of July 1944. The landing craft that carried us ashore from a British cargo vessel had dropped its front ramp after we slid up onto the shingle of the beach at high tide. We had all our gear in hand and on our backs, including some new rifles –M1 Garands—we'd picked up somewhere in England. A full field pack contained the normal stuff the soldier carries with him away from the base camp—blankets, shelter half, mess kit, socks, and underwear. We also carried a duffel bag of uniforms, socks, and underwear. The wreckage of D-Day, June 6, was still on the shoreline, and behind me out in the English Channel, I saw hundreds of ships—some moving, some dead in the water, too many only partially visible; smoking, scattered refuse of once proud warships.

It was sobering to realize how close the war was. Once on the beach, we formed a ragged column and marched through the debris, still there, from the initial assault on June 6.

Helmets, jeeps, tanks, landing craft, ration boxes, life belts, and crates of every size—the junkyard of war was there at the edge of the sea. The only apparent effort to clean up the beach was the removal of the bodies of the soldiers, sailors, and coast guardsmen who'd died at the water's edge or washed ashore.

This was still a narrow beachhead, and we continued across, then up a steep hill. The front, near Saint-Lô, was less than twenty miles away and the German Army was still trying to push our troops back into the English Channel.

Our little makeshift platoon struggled up the hill past more detritus: smashed German bunkers, pillboxes, and barbed wire that had been pushed aside or torn by Bangalore torpedoes. None of us had been in combat yet, but we were looking it in the face. The only things missing in the scene were the torn uniforms and bodies.

We were replacements for the line troops in the divisions that landed on June 6 and the days since. Casualties on D-Day had been great, but we would soon learn even greater in number were the dead and wounded in the hedgerow fighting in the Normandy countryside beyond the beach. Our ranks and files in the front lines were maintained at a fighting level by sending in new soldiers from the Replacement Depots. The Army used the terms "Reinforcement" and "Replacement" almost interchangeably. I didn't know which I was, but I would have liked the name "reinforcement" better. "Replacement" means that you are taking someone else's place, and you have a good idea what happened to the one you are replacing.

Whatever the name, there were 342,648 "reinforcements" in the 1st Army in the ETO during the war. (1)The U.S. Army system depended on a flow of men that started in training bases in the States. Men from these bases went out to depots and were "stocked", just like the supplies of food and ammo. Just as the ammo was expended and replaced, so were the front-line infantrymen. The riflemen went forward from the depots rather quickly.

Other types of soldiers waited until they were needed. Those who waited were the specialized technical men. During the "Bulge," however, most of these GIs were reclassified and rushed into the combat zone to fill the empty ranks in the Infantry. Their training in basic infantry survival knowledge was strictly "on-the-job". They either learned fast, or they died.

Our group was one of many gathered together from bases and camps in the U.S. and rushed overseas to take a place in the frontline divisions.

I had spent the previous one and a half years as a cadre platoon sergeant in Fort McClellan, Alabama. My job was to take new trainees and make them into something resembling soldiers. I had been drafted, trained at Ft. McClellan in basic infantry knowledge, and then had been kept at the base as Cadre' when my cycle moved out. The men (boys, really) I trained with went straight overseas to join the 45th and 36th Divisions in Italy. Many of them were killed on Anzio and at Salerno. I stayed to teach new men close-order drill, infantry tactics, the care and use of weapons, personal hygiene, guard duties, and military discipline. After a year and a half of training others, I decided to volunteer for a transfer. I didn't know where I would end up, but I knew that I wanted to move on.

I had thought at one time about volunteering for the newly formed Paratroops. I heard, though, of one of our lieutenants who did just that; he was transferred to Ft. Benning, GA, and went into Jump School to be an airborne trooper. One of his first training jumps was from the high static line tower. The trainees jumped attached to a bungee cord. Unfortunately, his cord broke, and so did his neck. That news dampened the enthusiasm of some of us who had once looked forward to the adventure and the extra $50 per month pay.

I did try for the Air Cadet program; took the test and passed with "first place," was accepted and then quickly rejected because I hadn't been a U.S. citizen for at least six months. I had become a citizen just a month before, courtesy of the U.S. Army. It had never occurred to me that I was not an American citizen before being drafted. I had lived in America as long as I could remember. But looking back over my life, I realized I had never applied for citizenship. I was much like the so-called "Dreamers" of today.

My brother, Martin, and I were born in Scotland. Dad was a marine engineer, sailing the seven seas. Well, not all seven, but mainly to India and Africa. He sailed on Ellerman Line ships working in the engine room, helping to keep the ship running properly and on time.

We rarely saw him because each voyage took months of sea time. The vessels were medium sized cargo ships, and they went where the cargo was, picked it up, and took it where it was supposed to be.

He was offered a shore job at one point—in Kenya, Africa—and we nearly went there. But he didn't take the job, and finally signed off the ship in Canada. He followed many other Scot engineers including his older brother, my Uncle, in going to work for the Ford Motor Co. in Detroit, and entered the United States on, of all things, the Detroit Ferry.

Around 1926 Dad left Ford to travel to New York to start working for the Hudson Engineering Co., a marine repair business, in Hoboken, New Jersey. My mother, brother, and I left Scotland in 1927 to join him, sailing on the *T.S.S. Cameronia.* The T.S.S. stands for Twin Screw Steamship.

We traveled in the dead of winter, and the crossing was just as rough as the trip on the Dominican Victory ship would be, eighteen years later, coming home from the war in 1945.

Dad was still with the Hudson Engineering Co. repairing ships when Britain went to war in 1939 with Germany. As the war progressed, the German submarines took a huge toll of ships in Britain's supply line, and dad was working night and day to repair the ships that managed to make port and get them back out to sea. Many of his shipmates, who were still sailing, were on ships torpedoed by the Germans, and lost at sea.

We listened to the radio and read the papers for news about the war. Our cousin, Jack MacKay, who was in the Royal Air Force, was killed. My mother's half-brother, Bill MacLean and his wife, Peggy, went into an air raid shelter in Clydebank, Scotland, and came out after three nights and days of bombing by the German Luftwaffe, to find everything they owned blown to bits. The Germans were trying to hit the Scottish shipyards that lined the banks of the River Clyde.

Mother joined a knitting circle and made gloves, scarves, and wool Balaclava helmet liners for the soldiers and sailors of the United Kingdom.

Our family was very much aware of the war and knew that the U.S. was going to be in it soon. Dad's brother was Chief Engineer on a ship in the United Fruit Co. His ship, the *S.S. Talamanca*, was commandeered by the U.S. Navy Reserve. He told us tales of seeing U.S. Navy warships attacking German submarines on the high seas.

After graduating from high school, I went to work at Dad's marine repair company, Hudson Engineering Company. The shop was very busy repairing ships and doing war work. Next door to the Hudson was the Ferguson Propeller Co. They made large, cast iron propellers for landing craft, and they gave them to us still hot from the mold. Charley Bothe, the machinist, and I put them onto an overhead crane, then hauled the "wheels" (in marine language, propellers are called wheels) to the rear of the shop where the big Bore Mill sat. Our job was to bore out the hub to a fine finish, where the ship's propeller shaft would fit.

The work was hard and long, but we knew we were doing something for the war effort.

December 7, 1941 was a Sunday. My friend, Dick

Burns, and I walked to our buddy, Jack Hogan's house, and there we heard about Pearl Harbor. The news had just come over the radio. We listened to the reports for a few minutes, then hurried back to our homes.

My mother got a little weepy when we talked about this new war. She knew that my brother Martin and I were at the right age to be called up, and the draft was already in operation. I was 17, and Martin was 19. She had seen plenty during the 1914-1918 war in Scotland when Dad served in the army and fought in France and Belgium. Of course, we told her not to worry, we'd be OK.

The next day at work I heard President Roosevelt declare that a state of war existed between us and Japan.

The country began to tense up and prepare for war. Security was ratcheted up. The Coast Guard came to Hudson Engineering and the other marine shops and issued Captain of the Port Identification Cards to all of us who worked on ships.

All my friends were thinking about the immediate future. We knew it held service in some branch of the military, but we didn't know which one. Without telling our parents, Dick Burns and I went to the Navy and Marine recruiting offices. At each one, they said, "We'll take you" to my friend, Dick, but "We won't take you" to me. I was a British subject, and the U.S. armed services weren't taking foreigners yet.

Dick decided to enlist in the Army and have the advantage of choosing where he would serve. He picked the Signal Corps. I signed up for the Draft. My brother was called soon after, and he went into the Army Quartermaster Corps. Hogan went next, into the Army Air Corps. Elbrecht, Reiss, Larson, Warren Poling—all my friends—one after another went into the services. They were eager to go and ready to do their bit. None of us remotely thought about not joining up. In fact, we dreaded the idea that we might be classified 4F. That would mean that we were not healthy enough to serve our country. If I remember correctly, all of us were 1A, and we all signed up "for the duration."

Eventually I was drafted into the Army Infantry, and as mentioned earlier, I became an infantry instructor in Alabama. Even though I didn't qualify for the Army Air Corps due to my recent change in citizenship, I still wanted to move on from Ft. McClellan, and that meant getting on a list of volunteers to transfer out. Once Headquarters had enough men on the list, the orders were cut, and we were on our way.

We traveled by steam train to Ft. Meade, MD, near Washington DC. At this post, we waited to get on another list. On the train, I'd met other "noncoms" (non-commissioned officers) who felt the same way I did. We were tired of the routine of doing training, cycle after cycle, and not having any experience of war. I don't think any of us were anxious to start digging foxholes in a combat zone, but we did want to do something that was real and closer to the "war effort". If it involved joining a division in combat, I think we were vaguely ready for that. Unfortunately, we didn't know what we didn't know.

I buddied up with several other sergeants during the trip to Ft. Meade. We were together for the next few weeks and had a lot of laughs during our time together. One sergeant, Bob Nelson, became a good friend. He was from Chester, PA, not too far from Brooklyn, and we really hit it off. Bob was a level headed, clear-thinking guy and a good soldier.

After several days at Meade, the lists were posted, and we boarded a train to Camp Myles Standish, near Boston. At this time, we knew we were going overseas, because Standish was an embarkation point. Any thoughts of a comfortable post in the U.S. disappeared. The sweat started when we saw that some of the replacements that had arrived ahead of us were being issued new khaki sun-tan uniforms. This meant that they were going to the Pacific. We rejoiced when our group was lined up, marched over to the quartermaster's shed, and were issued new olive-drab wool uniforms. Yeah! We were headed to Europe—the ETO, the European Theatre of Operations. We were going to fight a civilized war on the plains of Europe, not in the bug-ridden jungles of the Pacific islands. We were happy.

Then, we were slightly unhappy: the plan for June 6, "D-Day", was announced, and we were still in camp in the U.S. We feared the war would be over before we got there. Most of us wanted to see some action—not a lot of action, but *some*.

Boston wasn't too far from our camp, but none of us were given passes. We had to stay close to the base because the process of getting the replacements into the proper channels was under way. Somewhere in Washington, the Army Replacement Training Center in the War Department was making its shipping lists, and names of the men in my small group started to show up on the bulletin boards.

One after another, our buddies shipped out. Bob Nelson, two other sergeants, and I stayed together though, and finally we boarded the U.S. Coast Guard ship *USS Wakefield* in Boston.

The *Wakefield* was a large converted ocean liner. She was the *SS Manhattan* in pre-war times and had been taken over as a troop ship after catching on fire and being refurbished. I learned later that she took the U.S. troops to Europe on voyage after voyage, bringing German prisoners to the U.S. on her return trips.

The Atlantic was fairly calm during the crossing, and I was glad that I didn't get seasick. Every other time I had been on a big ship I had been deathly ill. Maybe I had too much to do on this trip. We sergeants were given twenty-five to thirty men each per "platoon", and we had to get them to various events and assignments like cleaning the decks, compartments, and, particularly, the latrines (or the "head", as the Coast Guard called it). These were not pleasant jobs, but the GIs had to do them, and not necessarily with a smile. That's why we sergeants had to be there to enforce the order. However, most of the platoons were made up of green draftees, so they didn't grumble much.

We disembarked in Liverpool and were trucked to a camp somewhere in England. There, we went through a series of inspections. All our equipment was laid out in the proper form and counted and re-counted. Tents were our barracks and although the calendar said it was summer, a coal stove kept us warm during those first damp, cool days.

Two days later we moved to another British camp closer to the English Channel, and this time we slept in ancient stone barracks. Instead of a G.I. cot, we were supposed to sleep on British army-issue straw mattresses shaped like mummies. These awful so-called mattresses were shaped in the outline of a man, and not a large one. They only allowed the sleeper to lie on his back. Roll over and you're on the floor; the upper bunk bed was particularly precarious. Fortunately, we only had to spend one night on these.

Somewhere, orders were cut for us to move forward, and the big trucks rolled up to take us to a seaport on the Channel. A small British ship waited for us at the dock, barrage balloons tethered overhead, and steam up. Nelson and I were the only remaining members of the group that had left McClellan. All the others had been put on different lists and were following their own paths on the way to new units.

At the dock, we put on our packs, shouldered our duffel bags, and climbed aboard. The trip across the Channel wasn't expected to be long, so we were not assigned to bunks. Instead, we were in compartments where we sprawled on the deck and waited for the next order.

The Channel crossing was uneventful and quick. As we

approached the Normandy shore, we were numbered with chalk on our helmets and told to go to designated boat stations where landing craft were waiting. The boats were hung on davits, special cranes alongside our ship's hull used to lower the small boat to the surf below. We just had to step over the rail and take a place in the small boat. Of course, with packs on our backs and duffel bags to carry, it wasn't an easy step.

After the boats were loaded they were lowered to the water, unhooked from the ship's lines, and we were off toward the beach. At the time, we didn't know that it was Omaha Beach. With our duffel bags slung on one shoulder and packs on our backs, we stepped out of the landing craft onto the shale of the French shoreline.

Marching inland a mile or so, we arrived at a field with pyramidal tents grouped along one side. Some noncoms came out and told us to take it easy, so we sat on our packs, smoked a cigarette or two and waited. And waited. And waited. Nothing happened. But this wasn't unusual. We all had been in the Army long enough to expect the old "hurry up and wait" routine.

At mid-day, we were marched down the road to another field. There we met some interesting GIs. These men were on their way back to their units at the front; nearly all of them had been wounded, injured, hurt, or lost. We were the green rookies, and they had all been in—or close to—combat. One G.I. had a fresh pink scar on his neck. Another had a long mark on his forearm. We mixed together with these fellows in the tents and the mess lines.

CHAPTER THREE
Beyond the Beach

The men on the way back to their units had worn their uniforms unchanged for a month. Some had caked, dried mud on their shirts and pants. Our boots were new and clean; theirs were not.

There was one other big difference. They were apart from us; they had been at the front. They had really been "to war". In the Civil War in 1863, these men were said to have "seen the elephant" , referring to seeing something outrageous, that they'd never seen before. We, our little band, were not in the holy circle yet. The wounded replacements didn't have to say anything about their experiences or actions. They knew they were different, and so did we.

We moved to another field closer to the front. This time we had no tents. We dug foxholes—just shallow trenches, really, only deep enough to sleep in. At night we covered ourselves with blankets and a shelter half. The weather was warm and not uncomfortable, but the nights were cool. During the day we sat by our foxholes, talked, smoked, and waited. Our group got smaller every day, as GIs were called out of our ranks and sent to their permanent units.

I don't know how far we were from the fighting, but we could hear shellfire, and while lying in our holes at night, we could feel the rumbling vibrations when the biggest shells hit the earth.

I was deep in my foxhole one night, staring up at the stars, when the thought came to my mind, "What the hell am I doing here?" Until then all my thoughts were focused on the job of getting to the war, and now the war was very close. I was in France, deep in it, and about to get into real fighting. Why was I asking the question now?

"Bed-check Charlie" stopped the introspection as he droned overhead. He was a pilot in a German plane that came over every night and occasionally dropped a few bombs. The engines made a weird wavering sound because they were unsynchronized, or so we were told. But I couldn't believe the German mechanics would let the plane fly with the engines like that every night. This night he dropped a chain of flares and was probably taking pictures. The lights made me stop what I was thinking, and I put it off for another time.

Our replacement group stayed in the field for several days. We talked and walked around the area and explored the smashed jeeps and tanks that were left from the initial invasion. Some men started printing their hometowns or states on the back of their field jackets. Bob Nelson had me print in block letters, "Philly Kid," on his. Like the other fellows, he wanted to advertise his home town.

For souvenirs, I cut a piece of fabric from a smashed army glider that had come in on June 6, and some silk from a U.S. parachute still hanging from a tree. I sent these to my younger brother, Bill, back in Brooklyn.

The Army mail delivery was amazingly good. I learned later that there was a mail detachment on Omaha Beach on D+2 (two days after D-Day). Our mail came through to us with little or no delay, even to our wandering replacement unit. How the Quartermaster (QM) found us was the amazing part.

We actually had mail waiting for us when we first arrived in England. Some of it was V-mail and some regular envelopes, but it got to us. V-mail was the microfilmed letterforms that put in our hands a 3"x4" copy of the original. In every army unit, mail call was the day's highlight.

We waited in our field with mixed feelings. The replacement lists were called each day, and Bob Nelson, the few sergeants that came over with us, and I were still waiting. We wanted to get our assignments to a real unit in a Division, but we also knew it would mean we were headed for combat. What we had heard about the fighting in the hedgerows - and had seen in the wounds of the other soldiers - didn't make us eager to run up to the front.

The front, however, came to us one night. Bed-check Charlie droned overhead just as we bedded down in the late evening twilight. He had become a routine, and no one paid much attention to him until we heard a rushing, tearing sound, and then two loud explosions. He had dropped a couple of bombs that landed just a few hedgerows away. It was pure luck, but he hit a truck on the road and killed two GIs. A few of our group went to the scene the next morning. When they came back and described it, what they seemed to find most remarkable was that the bodies had been taken away, but there remained a G.I. boot with a foot still in it. Little did they know the horrors they would soon face.

That evening we were sitting around a foxhole chatting and telling stories when we heard a roaring airplane engine. Someone shouted, "It's a German!"

As we jumped up we could hear machine gun fire, and again somebody shouted, "He's strafing!"

I said, "Christ, I don't have my helmet" and started running along the hedgerow to get my helmet from my foxhole. Nelson yelled, "Jim, get mine too!" I ran the 100 feet, grabbed the two helmets, and ran back. By that time, the German was over the horizon and gone, and we were left laughing at my stupid helmet run. None of us had even seen the German plane, but we sure knew he was there.

One morning, probably the day after the single German plane raid, more airplanes went over. This time, we could see them, and they were ours. I could see groups of P-47s, B-25s, and many B-24s. We soon lost count of the number of planes. The next day was similar, but this time the planes were predominantly B-24s. Wave after wave went over at about two or three thousand feet. The stream of bombers seemed endless, and while we watched, we could hear the heavy thump of bombs exploding just to the south of our position.

This, we learned later, was part of Operation Cobra, the twenty-three hundred plane bombing run that allowed the U.S. ground forces to break out of Normandy. The bombers smashed the German lines, but also killed hundreds of GIs when the bombs fell short.

What remained of our replacement group was finally assigned to permanent units. Trucks rolled up to our field, names were called, and we packed our duffel bags: we were off to the real war. Bob Nelson, Frank Lane, and I learned on the truck that we were going to the 3rd Armored Division. We looked at each other. What did we know about armor and tanks?

The answer: back in the states during training we had a light tank run over a foxhole that we were in, to demonstrate that digging a deep foxhole could save your life.

That was it.

When we reached an assembly point, we de-trucked and were told that Bob Nelson was going to "F" Co. of the 36th Armored Infantry, and Sgt. Lane and I were going to "E" Co.

At the E Co. CP (Command Post), the First Sergeant said that I would be taking over the 2nd Squad of the First Platoon. I would be a Squad Leader. I was also a Car Commander, because I was in charge of a squad of twelve soldiers, and we rode together in a "car" called a half-track. Our unit was the smallest group of men in our Division; we were at the bottom, or out in front, which is one way to look at it. There were five squads in our platoon, and three platoons in our company—E Company.

E Company was one of three companies in the 2nd Battalion—the other two were D Co. and F Co. In the 1st Battalion and 3rd Battalion, the companies were A, B, C, and H, I, J respectively. These three battalions made up the fighting force of the 36th Armored Infantry Division.

I was "home" at last. I hate to say it, but the men of that squad are, for the most part, lost to my memory. There are a great number of events during my time with the 3rd Armored that are crystal clear, but the names and faces of most of the men in the squad in Normandy are gone. Sure, there was Vories, my driver, and there was Deering, and "Recon," who became lost and was picked up by the 83rd Recon, hence, the nickname thereafter. There was Steve Serbin who died when we hit the Siegfried Line and Pitzer and Plummer who joined us as replacements later. The rest I can't remember.

But I do remember the lack of warmth in my new squad. They were cool and careful in their greeting, and I could understand that. They had been in combat for a short time, and I was the green hand—but I outranked them. I was the one that had to be tested, and my stripes didn't mean a thing until I had proved to them that I was their leader.

I met them alongside a hedgerow where my new "home" was parked. Home was a half-track, an M3A1, manufactured by the White Co. She carried one .50 caliber and two .30 caliber machine guns. Two big wheels were up in the front, and back where the rear wheels would be on a truck were tank treads instead, thus she was a half-track. Her name was Eleanor, and her identification number was E-12. The name was stenciled in white on the door, and the number was on the side panels.

It was a hot dusty day, and I was thirsty. A Jerry can on the back of the half-track held cider, the men said. I took out my canteen cup and half filled it with the cider and took a big gulp. My knees nearly went out from under me; I thought someone had hit me. It was made of apples all right, but the hard way—it was Calvados, 100+ proof and pure lightning.

The Tech Sergeant, Jim Cofer, came over and briefed me on the situation. The Division had entered combat at Villers Fossard and had been fighting since June 19th. He said we were part of Combat Command "B" and that we usually worked with the 33rd Armored tanks. He didn't say how to work with the tanks though. I figured I'd just have to watch and learn.

Then I met Lt. Hall, our E Company commanding officer. His full name was Almiron P. Hall, and he was slim and cool; a good-looking officer. We sat on the ground next to a hedgerow and he asked me about my background. I told him about Fort McClellan and my civilian life. He asked me if I had any questions. I had many, but I guess I didn't want to show him how ignorant I was, so I asked him a few silly questions before he was called away. I knew I didn't make a good impression on him. He was the only officer I met, and I later learned that all the other platoon leaders were killed in the previous weeks. Later, during the Battle of Mortain, he crawled along the foxhole line after a bad shelling, looked down at me in my hole, then smiled and said, "Glad to see you're still with us, Cullen."

After that first brief exchange with my new C.O. an alert came down and we were told to pack up and move out—on foot. Somewhere along the line I had been issued an M1 rifle. I think it was in England where we had to clean it of Cosmoline, the waterproofing grease. I had been hoping to go to a rifle target range to zero the weapon in before we went into combat, but it didn't look like that was going to happen. Someone said that if you got close enough, zeroing in didn't matter. Real close, and the sights didn't matter either.

The regiment was off the line when I joined it, but that didn't last long. The bombing of the German lines had allowed our 3rd Armored and the 2nd Armored to break out of the hedgerows to start the run across France. That, of course, was in the days ahead. Now we were trying to overcome the resistance that still existed in the fields south of Saint-Lô. The word came along to get ready to move out.

We weren't moving out in our half-tracks though—we were to climb onto the 33rd Armored tanks, Sherman M4s, and ride the back deck. The squad got on board, all squeezed together. I went up near the turret where the tank commander was in the open hatch. I thought the tanker and I would be discussing tactics and maneuvering, but he just ignored my men and me. (I found that that was the case, in general, for the rest of my war. The tankers fought their battles and we fought ours, and only occasionally did we work together, when they really needed us.)

My small squad (there were only seven or eight, not the twelve that were called for in the table of organization) wore raincoats folded on the back of their cartridge belts. Over each of their shoulders there was a bandolier of rifle ammo, and a light musette bag with K and C rations. We all had canteens of water and a medical pack on our belts. We were not heavily loaded; we were ready for running, crawling, and moving.

Our tank rolled along in a column with the rest of the tank platoon on a narrow road between two low hedgerows. Some shells started to come in with a whistling roar, exploding in the fields near us. I realized I was getting very close to real combat. Shell after shell arrived, landing all around us but we kept going through the smoke and dust. Then there was an extra loud explosion at the front of our tank, and it stopped. The crew started to climb out of their hatches and I grabbed the tank commander's arm and shouted, "What's going on?"

"We were hit by a Panzerfaust," he said.

"A what?"

"A Kraut bazooka" he shouted back.

We jumped down, crossed into the fields, then crouched along the hedgerow. By that time all the tanks had stopped, and our infantry platoon was assembling and moving on with the attack—without the armor.

This was my first combat experience and I wasn't leading the squad—just following what the others were doing and keeping my eyes open. The first squad led by Tech Sgt. Cofer and the C.O., LT Hall, crossed into the adjoining field. I spread out my men on either side of me and followed the leaders as they went forward. We went through holes torn in the hedgerows to the next square field, which again was bordered by hedges.

We had been going forward for about twenty minutes when I heard a terrible screaming roar. I knew it wasn't good when I saw all the men ahead of me going flat on the ground. I crouched down as the screeching grew louder and closer. Then the explosions started in the field to the left of us. Each scream ended in an enormous crashing blast. These were German "screaming meemies," six-inch diameter rockets launched from a carriage that looked like a pipe organ. Six rockets were fired at the same time, and they all landed and exploded within seconds of each other.

Something hard smacked into the stock of my rifle where I held it near the ground. A couple of inches closer and I would have had my first Purple Heart from a piece of hot German shrapnel.

When the screaming meemies stopped, we continued the attack - not that I knew where we were going, but I knew someone must have an attack plan with a phase line or an objective to reach. We couldn't see where we were headed because our world was the square field we were in. In the sunken roads between the hedges, the world was even narrower and smaller.

The attack pressed on. My squad followed with all heads swiveling to right and left and rifles at the ready. The Germans could have been in the next field over the hedgerow and we wouldn't have seen them. Each field was isolated.

We did see some young French men, though. They came out of a small patch of trees as we passed by. We shouted a question at them: "Les Boches, avez vous seen any? Allemand? German?"

"Mais non—no Allemand" they said as they shrugged their shoulders. We kept going.

Two minutes later we heard the whistle and rush of shells coming in at us. Three or four high explosive shells hit the field and hedges, but no one was wounded. We felt somehow that our French friends had pinpointed our position to the Krauts.

The attack speeded up after that. We ran and stopped, then ran again, and then were told to sit tight. We didn't sit; we flattened out on the ground.

The word came back that we had called for artillery, and it was on its way. Sure enough, the sound of our own shells whizzed overhead. Some of the first shells were WP—white phosphorous—Willie Peter, the marker shells. Two of them were short and they landed too damn close to us for comfort. WP put up a nice white smoke, but the particles from the shell burned anything they hit, particularly skin. They were deadly because the particles burn through the skin and into the body. They can't be extinguished with water.

We pressed on in the same general direction. I hoped somebody had a map and compass and knew how to use them. It was a hot sticky day. Running in the shade of a hedgerow was better than being in the open field, where it was both hot and dangerous.

Then I saw my first German artillery shell. We were crouching along a hedgerow and stopped when we heard incoming shells. One banged into our field, and another went over the hedgerow into the next field and exploded, throwing dirt all over us.

The next shell was a quick dark shape that flashed across my vision and slapped into the hedge. It was about two feet ahead of one of my men, who was about five feet from me. We froze in absolute fright, waiting, waiting. Slowly we realized it was a dud; it never detonated. But we got out of that field in a hurry, and on the run.

As we crossed another hedgerow and another field, the word came up to us to hold our position. We threw ourselves down in the shadow of the hedge and just lay there, physically and mentally exhausted. We hadn't seen the enemy, but he had sure let us know he was out there.

Most of the squad fell asleep immediately (a strange side effect of battle), but some of us started to dig in. A hole in the ground is an infantryman's best friend, especially during a shelling. After I had dug a decent hole, I woke the men who were sleeping and told them to dig.

Toward dusk we received orders to move out. We assembled in a field about two miles away. Again, we relaxed, smoking and sleeping and wondering what was happening. Again, we dug in. To this day, when I smell fresh dirt I instantly think of those foxholes in France and Belgium.

I thought, "So *that* was combat!" It had been a long, confusing, and dangerous day. It wasn't like training maneuvers in the States. During those "play at war" exercises at Ft. McClellan, we knew the plan ahead of time; where we were supposed to go and what we were supposed to do. It was planned and scripted, and we acted out our parts.

This "combat" in France was strange and confusing. Our unit moved forward—I suppose toward the enemy, and we kept alert looking to see a gray uniform, but there were none. Of course, with the hedgerows around the small fields, we might have been within ten feet of a

German squad and not have known they were there. The nice part was that *they* didn't know we were close either.

Our brief "R&R" - rest and recreation - didn't last long. South of us near the village of Mortain, the Germans were about to launch a counter-attack aimed at breaking through the American lines.

Long after the war, around 1985, I read about the campaigns in Europe in an attempt to find out where I was during 1944 and 1945. I had a vague idea of the general location of my Division, but no details.

Reading about Mortain in 1985, I learned the general conclusion of historians was that Hitler had decided to commit his 7th Army in a counter-attack into our lines. The intent was to disrupt the supply lines of the U.S. First and Third Armies. Those two armies were running across Normandy and Brittany after the Cobra breakout, and Hitler thought that he could call a halt to our armored columns with his surprise attack.

Some history books say that General Omar Bradley, head of the 12th Army Group, was forewarned of the attack by information picked up by Ultra, the code-breaking mechanism associated with Enigma. Other books say no, General Bradley did not know of the attack beforehand; that it took him by complete surprise and the fact that the 30th Division and parts of the 3rd Armored and 2nd Armored were in the line was pure luck, and not by design.

No matter what the reason, we were there. Our company was with Combat Command "B," and we were told to get ready to move out. Our orders came by radio to regiment, then to battalion, and then to company. The platoon leader's runner was the man to bring us the "word", and the word was to go forward, get to an objective unknown to us, dig in, and be prepared.

My platoon led the advance across the hedgerows and fields in a column.

The day was hot and dusty, the sun bright and glaring,

and we were tired, thirsty, and hungry when the order came up to halt. I spaced the men of my squad about five feet apart, close to the hedgerow that was nearly four feet high with matted branches across the top. Some K ration boxes and jerry cans of water were brought up as we dug our foxholes.

I walked along the line to make sure the men were digging in well. We didn't know whether we were staying in the position or, as usual, moving out as soon as the hole was finished. But we had to assume that we would be in place for the night.

As I checked on them, I was aware that I barely knew the men in the squad. I knew enough about them to call them by name, usually the last name, and not to shout, "Hey you, soldier" but that was about it. Eventually, I did get to know a little about each man, but not much. We never sat around a campfire and exchanged histories. Bit by bit we learned something about each other, but the most important things to me were whether the man was reliable and trustworthy, not where he came from. We learned about each other through actions, not words.

That night, I posted guard. One man had to be alert and awake at all times from sundown to first light. We did this by taking the hours of darkness and dividing them by the number of men in the squad. If the hours of dark in the European summer were eight hours and we had eight men, each man was on guard for an hour. Of course, this was only true if there was no action; if there was shelling and German activity, then everyone was up and alert.

In the field that night, we slept in our holes without blankets or shelter. We were tired, and sleep came easily. It was also the last night of undisturbed rest.

When morning and first light arrived, the platoon was wide-awake and ready. There had been shelling in the distance with some small arms fire, but nothing in our area. We ate some K's for breakfast, then took our shovels and did our toilet duty by digging a hole and then covering our waste. This we learned in basic training, and we found it was something the German soldiers never did. We concluded that they were never properly toilet-trained.

We didn't know where the Krauts were, but we hoped somebody did. The morning was spent digging more dirt out of the foxholes, because it appeared that we were not moving out right away. More rations and water were brought up, and we basked in the sun and waited.

The word came up to us that CC "B" was detached from the division and had been attached to the 4th Division. CC "A" had been attached to the 1st Division in the attack and occupation of the village of Mortain.

On August 6, the night that we built up our line at the hedgerow, our unit was reassigned to the 30th Division. We were to fight with the 119th Infantry Regiment of that Division. At least those were the plans of someone up at First Army. All we knew at our level was that we were waiting for something to happen.

The main battle seemed to be just to the south of us. We could hear the level of shell explosions mounting, and also the noise of our own artillery roaring and whistling overhead increased. Our guns sounded a dull bang behind us, and then came a whistling rush of the smaller caliber shells, then a louder tearing roar of the bigger 155s. We grinned at all of the "outgoing" headed toward the enemy!

CHAPTER FOUR
I'll Be Seeing You

The smiles stopped, though, in the middle of the day when I heard a "plunk" sound from beyond the hedgerow. I hesitated for a few seconds, and then realized it was probably a German mortar being fired. I yelled "Down" and dropped into my hole. Sure enough, an explosion blasted dirt into the air in the field on the other side of our hedgerow. The hedge protected us, but some dirt and rocks flew over to our side. A few more mortar shells came in a little closer. The result was that all of us along the line grabbed our shovels and dug even deeper into French soil.

We also maintained a watch at the hedge. Any barrage usually was designed to keep the enemy's head down while the ground attack went forward. I kept a couple of men on alert looking over the hedge, standing near the foxholes and ready to dive if we heard the plunk of the shell leaving the German mortar tube.

We rotated the guards, but no enemy appeared. The sun beat down on us. We ate when we could, relieved ourselves when we could, and just waited.

The mortars started again, and this time some landed in our field. The first shells hit the field in front of us and marched across the hedge into the one we occupied. All the men stayed down, but as soon as the shelling stopped, we were all up on the hedgerow with the safeties off on our rifles. The Germans didn't come.

The days passed, and which days and dates they were we didn't know. The Germans had hit the 30th Division line with the 2nd Panzer Division and the 1st SS Panzer Division. Their attack went through the forward positions of the 30th and flowed around Hill 314 where the 120th Regiment was emplaced. The men on the hill were completely surrounded and cut off. Their position, though, gave them a wonderful observation post on all the surrounding terrain. They were able to call artillery fire on any German vehicles moving in the roads below them and were a thorn in the Germans' side.

In our part of the battle we could only see from hedgerow to hedgerow. It was a flat, narrow world, and it became a very noisy one. The Germans started to shell our position as if they were determined to soften us up and then attack. The mortars started again. A GI in the 1st Squad, along the line from me about twenty feet away, wasn't fast enough when the shells started dropping in. He was hit in the back and buttocks and was a bloody mess. We shouted for the Medics and soon they came running in a crouch, put him on a stretcher, and took him away.

The next barrage was heavier. Mortar shells were fired at the same time they threw in the heavy High Explosive shells. The cannon shells must have been 75 mm or 105 mm or bigger. They came in with a whistling roar and ended in huge blasts, with dirt and branches of trees flying everywhere. We kept our heads down and prayed that they couldn't get a direct hit on the foxhole.

The rain of shells lasted for ten to fifteen minutes at a time. Then there would be a pause when we could check for casualties, go to the John either right in the hole or crouched close to the hedgerow. We would grab a bite to eat from our "K" ration or "C" ration cans and have a cigarette. Then we could hear someone yell "Incoming!" and the hellish noise and concussion would start again.

A close hit near my hole would cover me with dirt and leave my ears ringing. We, all of us there in the line, kept our eyes squeezed shut and begged the Good Lord to stop the awful rain of steel. At the end of each barrage, we were exhausted from the tension and tightness of our muscles as we crouched down in the hole.

(Infantry running alongside hedgerows in Mortain, France.)

The greatest relief came at night. Both sides, German and American, eased up a bit when darkness fell. It was a time for probing patrols, an occasional shell, the rattle in the distance of a machine gun or one or two rifles being fired at shadows. If there is such a thing as a civilized war, then those nights at Mortain were just that.

First light brought the nerves and worry up again. We felt that we were sitting in a target area and wondering how long we could last. Some men didn't - or couldn't - take the terrible strain. They broke and were taken to the rear with exhaustion and combat fatigue, even though we hadn't done any actual fighting.

None of my men went back to the aid station, but the strain on them was tremendous.

More shells came crashing in. One or two were near us, but the biggest ones were off to our right along the company line. Shell after shell hit, and fires started in that wooded area. We didn't know it at the time, but a real disaster was taking place there. All we saw and heard from our position was some of our Sherman tanks and half-tracks burning from direct hits. They had been assembled in the woods and had been targeted somehow by the Kraut artillery. We thought maybe a French peasant said something that led to such pinpoint fire.

We learned later the extent of the tragedy. Our Regimental Staff had come together for a meeting to plan, we were told, a "joint attack for us and the 119th Regiment of the 30th Division." Our staff officers met in a small shed and were busy planning our forward movement when a large caliber shell hit the building. It entered the room, and then exploded. Our Battalion and Regimental Commanders were killed instantly. They were Lt. Col.Vincente Cockfaire and Col. William W. Cornog.

With our leadership gone, our part in the attack was cancelled. The 119th went ahead, but they didn't get too far.

The burning vehicles sent up black clouds of smoke, and the German artillery spotters targeted it. They poured in more steel, and we got our share in our corner of the battle.

We could hear the ammunition in the Sherman tanks exploding, or "cooking off". We could also smell the tanks - and their crews - burning.

The air was already bad with the stink of dead cattle. They were in nearly every field in Normandy, victims of the shelling from both sides. After the animals were hit and killed, they lay on their sides, bloated and big with their legs sticking up stiffly in the air.

The smell of the dead wasn't too bad when we were on the move, but now we were in the 1944 version of trench warfare. It was like 1914. The shells from the Germans came in, and our side sent shells out, but we still never saw the enemy. We crouched in our individual trenches. When it rained we needed duckboards to stand on like those used in the 1914 trenches, but we had none—we just stood in the mud and muck.

In a great Bill Mauldin cartoon, the British are supposed to have said, "You Yanks leave a messy battlefield." Of course, they were talking about the way we threw away gas masks, packs, duffel bags and other gear. During this Mortain battle, the area around our foxholes became a mess of empty "K" boxes and "C" ration cans. No one policed the area, so when we ate, the wrapping and empties were tossed onto the field. Some were ground into the mud, but most of it just accumulated in piles. The British would have loved the scene.

We had been in the line several days and no Germans had appeared. We could hear small arms fire in the near distance, and a lot of that was German. We could tell by the sound. Our machine guns had a slow, steady rate of fire. It was a "dut-dut-dut-dut", while the Kraut machine guns sounded like "brrrrrrp". We actually called one of their weapons, the MP 38 submachine gun, the "Burp Gun." We heard that if you were hit by the first bullet, you would also be hit with the next six. It was a fast weapon!

The distant firing meant that our troops were engaged with the enemy in a firefight, and maybe it would be our turn next. They just threw countless shells in our direction, but thus far no tanks or foot soldiers. Some of us actually were getting frustrated, bored, and angry. We were getting blasted by the German shelling, but we couldn't fight back.

Someone at Headquarters must also have wondered where the enemy was and sent down a message asking for information. Our Platoon T/Sgt. Jim Cofer got the request (order) and crawled along the hedgerow to my hole.

"Cullen, we need a patrol out to the front to see what is going on. Take some of your men and go across to the next hedge to take a look."

It was broad daylight and I thought it would be better to do that sort of thing at night. However, I was the new sergeant and I wasn't about to request a postponement until nightfall. I said, "OK I'll just take one man".

I shouted to one soldier down the line that I knew was an "old timer." I knew he had been with the Division in the States and that he was from the South. His name was Leo Deering—we called him "Chowhound". I don't know why. He picked up the nickname before I joined the squad.

I told him we had to go beyond the next field to see what was going on. He nodded, and I told him just to bring his rifle and a bandolier of ammunition. Again, he nodded.

Before we started, Chowhound and I both looked over the hedge into the next field. We saw nothing except the grass of the field and the next hedge. As usual, the hedges grew on all four sides of the field. Our eyes roamed the whole area; nothing moved or looked out of the ordinary. It was time to go.

After we got up onto the hedge, we jumped down into the field and crossed it. The grass was just above our knees as we ran.

About fifty feet out, in the middle of the field, the rapid stutter of a German machine gun came from our left front, and the snap and crack of the passing bullets told us that we were the targets. We both made a dive for the ground and got as flat as possible. Burst after burst of fire cracked near us and I knew we had to get out of there fast. The grass was good concealment, but it wouldn't stop a bullet.

I shouted to Chowhound to get him ready to move; then I heard a choking, rattling sound. I shouted again, "Chowhound. Chowhound!"

I got no answer—just the rattle from the grass about

three feet from me.

I knew he must have been hit and it sounded as if he was choking. I shouted for him a few more times, but there was no answer; then the choking sound stopped.

I decided I was going back. I yelled, "Cofer, I'm coming back, you hear?" I didn't want to get shot by my own men when I went over the hedge.

I waited until the end of the next burst of fire, then jumped and ran back through the field. I hit the hedge and dove over the top. Sgt. Cofer and the rest were waiting, and I didn't have to tell them what happened—they had seen it all.

After dark, Sgt. Cofer went out into the field and checked Deering's body; he had been hit in the head. Cofer then retrieved the ammunition and water. He couldn't find Deering's rifle in the grass.

At first light we again waited for any evidence of German activity. Nothing happened until some high explosive shells came flying in, on and off, during the morning. They harassed us with artillery. No one was hurt in our section of the line, but the constant shelling with no action on our part was getting to us. We hated being pinned down with the fear of sudden attack, but we started to hate the Krauts even more for not giving us a chance to hit them back. It was a game of "come out, come out, wherever you are, you bastards. Give us a clean shot at you."

Cofer came crouching along the line again in the heat of the afternoon. He always carried a Thompson and his helmet was distinguished with two bullet holes near the back. He had stuck his head around a hedgerow a week ago, before I arrived, and a German bullet nearly got him.

He sat by my foxhole, and we talked about Chowhound and what had happened to him. Apparently, we were facing a strong German defensive position. "They are masters at defending in the hedgerows," he said. "They dig holes through the base of the hedge, and each hedge has a soldier in it covering the field. You can't see them, but they can see you. Then they put machine guns in the holes at the corner of the field, covering it with cross fire. That's probably what hit Chowhound."

Then he said, "By the way, I have another job for you." I wondered if I was the only Sergeant available, or just the newest one, or maybe he didn't like me. In any case, he said, "Cullen, I need you to go back to the C.P. and get a couple of replacements. They were just brought up."

I asked whether it was the E Company or Battalion Regiment CP and where it was. He said it was the Battalion and gave me directions. "Go along this hedge until you get to a sunken road. Turn right in the road, go to the rear, and you'll find it. When you get there, tell them you're there for two new men. Be careful."

I took my rifle, climbed out of the hole and bent over in a crouch, then started along the line. Passing my squad and then another one, I found the sunken "road". It was a narrow cart path, lower than the surrounding fields, and bordered by high hedges. These were at least ten feet high and met overhead, making a shadowed tunnel. I started along this "road" just as a German barrage of H.E. came in.

I realized the sunken road was a pretty safe place to be. It was like a long World War One trench, and I enjoyed a safe rest there until the shells stopped.

I found the C.P. by asking every GI I met on the road and getting very vague directions. "Just go that way. I think it's a couple of hundred feet." The CP was a couple of officers with a radio and a box with maps and overlays on it. There were also some non-coms and GIs sitting idly on the ground.

Telling one of the non-coms who I was and what I needed, he said, "OK, wait over there" and pointed to the hedge by the road. I sat down opposite a T/Sgt. who was sitting and smoking a cigarette. I opened a K ration and started to grab a bite. We talked, and he said something about F Company and I asked him if he had been with F Company for long. He said that he had been with it back in the states, and then I remembered Bob Nelson, my buddy, had been assigned to F Company.

I asked the Tech if he knew a Sgt. Nelson and he asked how I spelled it. I told him, and he took a little black book out of his pocket. Thumbing through it, he stopped and then said, "Nelson, yeah, Robert. He got hit. He's had it. He was asleep in his foxhole when a tree burst got him— in the head." He closed the black book and looked at me. "You knew him?" I could only nod my head. "Tough" he said.

I didn't finish eating.

I sat there a minute, shocked, thinking about Bob, and then heard someone shouting, "E Company, where are you?" My two replacements were there. They were young, the same as me, maybe nineteen or twenty. I had just turned 21 two weeks previously. Both were clean—clean uniforms, clean shave, clean boots, and a clean pack. The only thing clean and bright about me was my rifle. I hadn't shaved or even washed since... I couldn't remember when. All I knew was that the last shower I had was in England, and that was more than two weeks ago.

The two men mumbled their names and rank, Private, and I told them, "We're going up to the 1st Platoon, so follow me, but not too close. And stay separated. Watch me, do what I do, and if I go flat—you go flat too."

We started along the sunken road, one behind the other. I thought we were near the line, when I heard the rush of "incoming." I yelled "Down" and hit the dirt. The shells blasted the area for three or four minutes, but we were safe in the low road. When it was over, I got them up and walking, but then there was another rush of shells going over, and my two recruits hit the dirt. I stood looking at them—me, suddenly the old soldier who knew the difference between "incoming" and "friendly" shells.

I got them to the line, Cofer took them away, and I

never saw them again.

Back at our position, I dropped into my foxhole and sat there, staring at nothing. Bob Nelson was gone! He had been hit! He was dead! The F Co. Sgt. didn't even know him; he was just a name in a black notebook. I don't know how long I sat there staring and thinking.

Bob was a good friend; steady, level headed, and a good soldier. We had met in the States, crossed the Atlantic together, gone through England, and now he was gone. My mind shied away from thinking about what happened to him after he was hit. I didn't want to know.

I thought about the times we'd had in Washington, D.C.: Getting passes from Ft. Meade, a bunch of us would taxi to D.C. to roam around and have fun. One place for drinks and fun was the International Club. It was a big lounge with tables and a bar. You could go up to the bar to buy a drink, but in 1944, D.C. law said you had to sit in a chair at a table to drink it. Another law said you couldn't go over to a lady's table and join her. Getting around that was easy. We could signal with our eyes or a nod of the head, or a quick question as we passed their table. They would leave and shortly after, we would take off, join the girls out on the sidewalk and come back in to the club, arm in arm. Everything after that was legal.

Bob was really attracted to a girl he met that night. Mine was just OK, but he went crazy, and couldn't wait to get back the next night and the next. We were waiting for travel orders to go overseas, and passes were easy. Each night we could get to the club and go through the routine.

The last night we were in Washington, we left the Club early and wandered down to the Potomac and separated. Bob and his girl went off somewhere, and my girl and I climbed up to the Lincoln Memorial (there were no guards then) and looked at the stars.

That day was our last in D.C.; we left by train for Camp Myles Standish in Massachusetts. It was close to Boston and was to be our port of embarkation. We were only there a few days, but letters started to arrive for Nelson from his girl. She was light haired, pretty, and smart; I think her name was Helen but I'm not sure. She must have written several times a day and Bob was doing the same thing.

Our orders arrived, and we boarded the Coast Guard ship USS WAKEFIELD in Boston Harbor and sailed for England. The WAKEFIELD was a fast ship, so we didn't go with a convoy. She sailed alone at full speed and zigzagged her way across the North Atlantic.

The second day after we arrived in Liverpool, the letters for Bob were called out at mail call. The rest of us got nothing. On the ship, we had kidded Bob about the letters and the girl, but he smiled and said, "You guys can go to hell—this is serious. I'm going to marry her". We told him he was nuts, and that he'd forget her when we got into France.

Back in Camp Myles Standish, we had started singing in the shower. We all showered the Army way—nine or ten GIs, all at the same time. We sang at the top of our lungs the then popular song, "I'll be Seeing You." It's a slow, gentle song, but we made it sound like a college drinking song, singing as loud as possible, laughing all the time at Bob because he was thinking of his Helen. "I'll be seeing you".

No, Helen, you won't, I thought. All you'll see is a returned pile of letters with "Deceased 10-08-44" handwritten on the front of the envelope.

As I was thinking of those days (which, incredibly, were only a month before), Sgt. Cofer came along the line and crouched by my hole. We talked about standing guard, the shelling, rations coming forward, and water. Then as he left, he said, "Oh yeah, the Topkick, Eubanks, took a bullet between the eyes" and then he left. I didn't know Eubanks; I'd never met him. I felt sorry he had been hit, but I felt a hell of a lot worse about Bob Nelson.

CHAPTER FIVE
Mortain

A little later, after more mortars and shelling, the word came along the line that we were to move out. No one said which way we were moving—would it be toward the Germans or away from them? Half of me wanted to attack them after all the crap they had thrown at us, but the sensible half said *hell no, move back out of range*.

Good sense prevailed. We were relieved from our position by some other dogfaces. Following the sunken roads back behind the line, we found our half-tracks. They were assembled in a wooded area about two miles back. E-12, Eleanor, looked good. She was parked in a field coiled with the rest of the platoon. Our driver, Vories, was taking good care of her.

The squad boarded the 'track', and we drove to a new field even farther back. Here we settled in and put the camouflage net over Eleanor. I broke the crystal on my watch when the radio aerial caught on the net, as I was helping put it on and the aerial hit my wrist. But just like a Timex, it kept on running and running.

We broke out the Calvados hidden in the Jerrycan and had a few sips of that powerful brandy. I got to know some of my squad then, and as usual, they were a mixed lot. I wish I could remember their names and faces, but they have nearly all faded.

The drink loosened us up, and we joked and laughed. Our hometowns were a source for jokes and kidding and ribbing. We didn't drink that much actually; we were all pretty young and none of us were drinkers. We were still learning the game. I suppose the relief of tension and fear multiplied the effect of the drink because we cried laughing over the silliest line or the stupidest joke. The battle was over, and we had been close to death, and we were high with adrenaline. We were still laughing as we dug shallow holes for the night. We took no chances and posted guards as usual.

The coolness the squad had shown me when I joined them initially seemed to have disappeared. They were very warm and friendly now. Perhaps my actions at the hedgerows had convinced them that I wasn't a bad guy. By taking that fatal patrol, they probably figured that I wasn't the type to avoid any duty that I might order them to do. I had seen the elephant.

The next morning, we were up at the crack of dawn and were surprised to get a hot breakfast sent forward by the kitchens. The food was in big canisters called Mermite cans. The eggs were fake, the Spam was cold, and the butter was fake also—we called it axle grease. It was designed not to melt under any conditions, and it didn't. But we appreciated the effort and ate it all with no complaints.

We cleaned our gear and lazed around until late in the morning when Lt. Hall, our Company Commander, called all the Sergeants to a corner of the field. He gathered us in a circle and then held up a bottle of Johnny Walker Red. He said, "We found this in the 1st Sgt. Eubanks bedroll. I think that we should have a drink on him and wish him well." We smiled as he opened the bottle and passed it around. We each took a drink and passed it on.

That's how I met the other squad leaders. We chatted,

passed the bottle, exchanged some stories about the last few days, and got to know what the other men looked like.

We were still talking when a runner came up to Lt. Hall and gave him a message. He read it and then told us to get ready to saddle up. "The Krauts are moving, and we are back on the road."

With the tank engines vibrating in our chests, and the sound of our half-tracks adding to the din, the Platoon moved out of the field in a column, the tanks to our rear. The road was dusty, and we quickly became hot and dirty. Still wearing the same uniforms we put on in England, we must have been a stinking crew, but no one noticed. Our hope was that we weren't going back into the hellhole we had all just left.

The column stopped, and we were assigned to one of the 33rd Armor tanks. To get aboard the tank you had to find a handhold, step on the tank track or bogey wheel, then haul yourself up onto the back deck behind the turret. We squeezed together and hung on to any place we could. In addition to us, the tankers had their rations, sleeping bags, and musette bags up there too. It was crowded. We also had to be aware of the turret, because if the gunner rotated it to bear the gun on an enemy, we had to move out of the way. There were no warnings from the tank commander. Our tank took us to a road junction and stopped. We were happy when we were ordered to set up a roadblock. We got off and I spread the squad along the edges of the roads. The other squads were dispersed on other crossroads. Sgt. Cofer came along and told us to dig in at the side of the road and get ready. He said, "There may be some Kraut tanks coming this way from Mortain. Keep alert."

That was the first time I heard the word "Mortain". I later learned that Mortain was the name of the battle we had been in all week.

Years later, someone asked me if I was at the Battle of Mortain, and I said we were just at a roadblock.

At the roadblock, we dug in in a defensive position and waited. I wondered what the hell we were going to do if a tank did come along the road. Our armament was one M1918 BAR machine gun and seven rifles; no bazookas, no rifle grenades. The BAR was a heavy, hand-held machine gun, and each unit had one man who was designated the "BAR guy", because it took a big man to be able to carry it. I guessed that we were supposed to be forward observers and our job was to warn the tank, which was behind us, if we saw any enemy coming down the road.

The fact that we were positioned between the tank's gun and the possible enemy also occurred to me. There was no communication between us and the tank other than an arm wave or one of us running back to the tank and banging on the hull. The only enemy we could stop by ourselves was the Kraut infantry.

We waited in the hot sun in our foxhole while the tankers roasted in their mobile oven. We ate K's, smoked, and slept, with some of the men on alert. No Krauts appeared.

Then there was a whistling roar from overhead. We all ducked into our holes, and then realized the noise was from aircraft. A flight of Royal Air Force Typhoons appeared overhead and started diving at an angle toward the ground ahead of us. Each airplane fired rockets in turn, then climbed away to circle overhead. The rockets disappeared behind a low hill two or three hundred yards to our front. Explosions and smoke rose as the planes came back and hit the targets again. More smoke came up, and we could hear muffled secondary explosions. We figured that was ammunition cooking off.

What the Royal Air Force was hitting we never knew, nor did we care, other than the fact that their targets hopefully were German tanks and trucks headed in our direction.

The smoke from this attack was still in the air when we

were called back to get onboard the tank. We rode to an assembly point. Once again, our half-track was waiting with the rest of the platoon, coiled around the edge of a field.

The squad took life easy for a bit. We ate, smoked, cleaned our weapons, slept, or did nothing but sit and talk. No shells were coming in near us, and there were no alerts or alarms. We watched large numbers of Allied planes flying over, happy they were ours.

I had a chance once more to look at my men as they lazed around the half-track; to think about them and how they would act in the next enemy encounter. The last week had not been a "fight" in any sense of the word. We took a pasting in the area we were defending, and that was about all. We did our job by holding and securing the flank of the 119th Infantry of the 30th Division. Our regiment took a great number of casualties, including the loss of the Headquarters staff, but it wasn't a pitched battle.

The next few weeks, I knew, would certainly see us in some real action, and I tried to evaluate each guy during this quiet period. Looking back over sixty-plus years, I can remember very few of the men. Others are just faint shadows. I can't remember their names or their faces. The number of men in the squad in Normandy is also something I can't remember. I'm pretty sure it never reached the twelve which our Table of Organization called for. Whatever the number, we got to "know" each other a bit during the lull. All the important facts came up; home state, hometown, and basic training. I listened to their talk and observed how they acted, trying to form opinions; although I figured that the way they talked now didn't really mean they would be steady in a firefight. The proof had to wait until we were back in action.

The rumble of tank engines started across the fields. The 33rd Tank Regiment was moving. We figured our order to move could come soon, and it did.

We loaded all our gear onto Eleanor and got moving

onto the road and into our place in the platoon column. Someone ahead of us knew where we were going, but we didn't.

From the angle of the sun, the column had to be headed north. Sgt. Cofer confirmed this when we stopped for something up ahead. He told us we were driving up to meet the Canadians coming south, and that, "if we get together, a bunch of Krauts will be trapped."

That was great; at least we knew the objective. Gunfire sounded up ahead, and then a few USAAF P-47 Thunderbolts came over and took turns strafing and bombing something further along our path.

When we started moving again, we entered the town of Couptrain; we quickly passed through it and were soon out in farmlands. A little beyond the town, the column stopped once more, and we coiled into a field. All around us, in the fields and on the roads was smashed and burned German equipment. There were trucks and little German jeeps called Kubelwagens. Bodies were still in the vehicles and lying in the road.

The squad climbed down from E-12 and broke out some K and C rations while sitting on the grass and waiting. I joined them. Nearby was a burning German assault gun. Its long gun tube was depressed, and I realized I was looking right into the muzzle; it was pointing right at me! If there was a shell in the breech, I figured that the fire would eventually make it "cook off." I moved.

I wandered off with a few of the other guys to look at some of the German equipment and to see if there were any souvenirs to be had. When we came back to our track, I saw a long fresh gash in the turf, exactly where I had been sitting. There *had* been a shell in the German gun, and it *had* fired.

Moving again, we saw that the land was changing from the low hills of Normandy with the hedgerow fields, to more open, flat farmland. The visibility reached to the horizon, and our tanks could maneuver and fight in proper tank fashion. Normandy's hedgerows had been a terrible series of obstacles for the heavy equipment.

We slowed and knew there was some fighting going on up ahead; we weren't called into it, but at least we were alert and ready.

Many times, we sat in the road by the half-track waiting for the armor up ahead to eliminate the strong point, go around it, or call us up to the front.

I was beginning to learn about tank warfare and how it differed from infantry fighting. Up ahead, the tanks were battering forward toward an objective. Their mission was to reach that objective and to smash through anything in the way or go around it. The by-passed enemy roadblock would then be attacked and hopefully reduced or eliminated by the following infantry regiments.

Our job, as Armored Infantry, was to work with the tanks up at the point and to protect them as they attacked toward their objective. Regular infantry, when attached to our Division, usually followed in trucks or on foot. Then these troops would use regular infantry artillery tactics to eliminate the problem.

FALAISE

When we parked in a field at nightfall, we could see that the clouds on the horizon were reflecting a white light. Then we heard that it was a Canadian method of night fighting. Anti-aircraft searchlights were aimed into the sky to reflect off the low clouds to illuminate the battlefield. I guess the Canadians found the method to be effective, and that the light enabled the Canadian infantry to see the enemy. But if you can see them, they can see you, too.

Our Combat Command B did some major fighting up in front of us, and they did close the gap in meeting the Canadian Army. Fifty thousand German troops were trapped and taken as prisoners. Unfortunately, many more slipped out of what would become known as the Falaise Gap.

CCB, with the rest of the Division, then went into a

bivouac area for some badly needed maintenance and reorganization. The Division had been in almost continuous action since June 29 and needed repairs to men and machines.

The platoon again coiled in a field with a good fifty-foot interval between each half-track. We learned that we would have a few days for repairs and maintenance, and I took the opportunity to learn more about the 2nd Squad of the 1st Platoon. Not that I wanted to know each man in depth and to become his closest buddy; however, I did want to know each man's ability to do a job in combat. Was he steady? Was he reliable? Was he a shooter or just an "observer", to put it charitably? Would he act in combat, or do nothing and freeze? I knew each man, including me, would be "scared shitless," but that was normal and common. We talked about how "really" scared each of us was in the Mortain shelling and tried to outdo each other with tales of our fright. Most of the rest period I watched the men interact with each other, and how they responded when given an order.

They were good men, a lot like the trainees I worked with at Ft. McClellan. Back there, I had a platoon of thirty-six men who were all green as grass when they arrived at the training company (A Company, 25th Battalion). They couldn't march in step or even walk in a straight line, but after eighteen weeks of Basic, they could walk straight and shoot straight too.

I got to know those men at Ft. McClellan pretty well in the barracks and on maneuvers. They all had been drafted yet didn't show any resentment in that event. However, many of them did not like the idea of being trained for the infantry. They wanted something more glamorous and less dangerous—like the Air Corps.

Here in Falaise, my men in the 2nd Squad were no longer trainees. The Army had put its stamp on them, and they knew how to act and behave as the Army said "…in a Military Manner."

(Cullen's squad on a tank somewhere in France.)

CHAPTER SIX
Northern France

After three days, the "saddle-up" order came, and we were off on the road again. The 3rd Armored Division's job was to catch the German Army, hurt him to make him run, and then catch him again. The Division rolled across France, out of contact with the enemy. We were like tourists, looking at the countryside as it rolled by. By the second day, the view became cloudy because our eyes were burning from the bright sun and the exhaust of the tanks and half-tracks. The dust we kicked up finished us. Our eyes were red, irritated, and sore; and so were we! The tankers all had been issued goggles with tinted sun glare lenses. We had none.

As they say, necessity is the mother of invention, and we managed to get our own glasses by searching through wrecked German tanks and half-tracks. The Krauts were issued beautiful little folding packets of goggles with dark lenses; they were neat and better than the big ugly G.I. issue anyway.

We caught up with German rear-guard troops as our column approached the River Seine. Our forward element, the 83rd Reconnaissance Battalion, took care of the light opposition and we rolled on. At the river we waited while the engineers threw a pontoon bridge across the water. When our turn came, Charley Vories, Eleanor's driver, edged our track onto the narrow steel treads and over the river we went. I knew we were near Paris, because the Seine passed through it, but we were not going there. I heard that the French Army had been given the privilege of liberating the city.

After the Seine, we had almost daily contact with the enemy. The Germans were running for home, but they were not the organized, disciplined enemy that had conquered Europe. They had lost thousands of men in the Falaise Gap. Some units that were streaming toward the German border had no officers and few non-coms; they were a mob in uniform. These troops usually surrendered when they saw our vehicles come down the road.

One day we were at the head of our task force. I was with the squad on foot doing some advance patrolling when five Germans came out of the brush on our right. They were surprised, and so were we. They dropped the bags they were carrying and stuck their hands in the air and then they smiled at us. "Kamerad" each man said as they walked toward us. I told my men not to fire and beckoned the Krauts forward. We had them throw down their helmets, pick up their packs, then sent them to the rear.

At one time I had thought of killing every German I saw as revenge for what they did to Bob Nelson, but by the time these five helpless soldiers walked out of the woods, I had lost most of that anger. I had seen a lot of German prisoners and dead bodies along the road and in the vehicles our Air Corps had hit in our advance, and now we were seeing much more of that. My anger was gone and replaced by a mild feeling of sorrow and pity for some of the men that we were chasing. Of course, there was also a healthy respect for many of the German troops, such as those we'd faced at Mortain. They knew how to fight, and we also knew that they wouldn't run forever. I learned years later, after the war, that they were the

German 2nd Panzer Division. At the time, we just knew we would surely see them again.

The pattern for our advance across Northern France was, to us, a simple one. We moved during the day then coiled into a "leaguer" at night. First light called for everybody to be alert with guns ready. Then the company order in the column would be passed along to us. The word might be that E Company would be third in the column in our half-tracks, or E Co. would be on board the E 33rd Armored tanks up front with nothing but the enemy to greet us. Or we might be alone on the road in our half-track with the tanks on a parallel road and 83rd Recon on another road. Each day was different according to the terrain and situation. Of course, attacking a town was another story. If the people of the town were clustered at the outskirts waving and throwing kisses and flowers, then we just rolled in, in tight column formation. If there were no French people in sight, then we knew the Krauts were waiting. Strategy and tactics took over, and we might go in from different roads or across fields, with our safeties off.

I guess we picked up our Division nickname, Spearhead, in the manner in which we were told about the order of attack. Our Tech. Sgt. Cofer usually went to get the word, and when he came back, we would ask, "Where are we?" He would sometimes answer, "Just call me Spearhead". Then we knew we were up front for the attack. The Spearhead name stuck.

(Cullen's squad in the distance on Eleanor, the E-12 half-track. Taken by Stan Rich from E-13.)

(Cullen's squad, 1st Platoon, 2nd squad, E Company, 36th Armored Infantry. Photo taken by Stan Rich, squad leader of 3rd squad, going across France, riding on Sherman Tank.)

Our company was spearheading one day, somewhere in France in our own sector, with 33rd tanks off to the left side and the other platoons of E Co. to our right. Sgt. Cofer came up to my track and said that the maps showed a deep rail road cut up ahead, and that we had to cross to the other side. The Krauts had blown the bridge over the railroad tracks and we had to clear the other side before the engineers could put in a new one for us.

The squads left the tracks and were spread at intervals along the road. We walked across the field—spread out. Bushes and shrubs grew along the edge of the railroad cut, giving us good cover as we approached. I placed the squad along the brush line then crept forward with a couple of the men to look at our problem. The rest of the platoon was off to our right. The cut had to be sixty feet deep, with the angle close to forty-five degrees. It would be easier to fall down the slope than to climb down and getting up the other side looked impossible.

Then we saw the real problem. There were German soldiers right in front of us. They were in a prone position, but we could see them clearly. They would rise up to look over the cut, so we knew they were aware of our presence. Not our squad, in particular, but they must have known the Division was approaching from the roar of the tank engines.

We talked it over. There were only a few Germans over there, probably part of the group that blew the bridge, and they had been left as rear guard. We decided to go ahead and attack. I passed the word along our line to fire on my shot, and to keep up suppressing fire. I told Steve Serbin and two other men that we would try to get across under the fire.

I took aim at one Kraut as he rose up to peer over to our side, and fired. The men then took it up and blasted away with BAR and rifle fire. I couldn't see any smoke or dust from returning fire, so we got ready to make the drop into the cut. I was really worried about the up slope. All the Krauts had to do was drop a grenade on us and we'd be done.

As we braced ourselves to go, I heard some sharp snaps and cracks. Those were bullets coming at us. I couldn't see the Germans firing, but we were taking fire from somewhere. We hit the dirt as the bullets cut the branches above us. "Holy Christ" I said. "Where the hell is that coming from? It can't be those guys over there."

"There it is" Recon yelled as he pointed to the left. "It" was our own tanks spraying .30 calibers from their bow guns. Three or four Germans jumped up opposite us from where they were lying flat in a depression and ran through the hail of bullets towards some woods. They made it.

We were mad but could do nothing about it. The tank platoon had found another bridge and had crossed, then turned right toward where we were attacking. We don't know whether they radioed their intention or just made the move on their own, but this incident was one of many in our "love-hate" affair with our armored brothers. We loved their cannon firepower, but we hated their noise and inability to see when they were buttoned up. Their noise attracted enemy fire and their blindness endangered us ground troops.

The tanks stopped their wild fire, and we went down in the cut and up the other side. It was a hell of a climb, and I'm sure we wouldn't have made it under fire.

At the top we found one dead German. The one I had aimed at. The bullet had hit him in the shoulder when he was parallel to the ground and went straight in.

When we assembled on the road again, we swore at the tankers, then forgot about it. There was nothing to be done.

Our column rolled through villages and towns, where laughing crowds waving glasses and wine bottles met us. They threw flowers, and young women (and some old), grabbed us for hugs and kisses. If our column stopped in a town, we would get off the tracks and mingle with the crowds. There was occasionally, however, an unfortunate incident. A girl would try to grab us for a kiss, but when we bent forward, the steel rim of our helmet would hit her just above the nose. We had to learn to be gentlemen and take off our hats as we liberated the French girls.

We passed many beautiful chateaux in park-like fields in France. Near one large one, the column stopped. Something up ahead, probably a river, was holding us up. Two people, a man and a woman, came from the building and strolled down to greet us. They were beautifully dressed. They glanced at us and then stared at our half-track.

We had picked up a lot of informal decorations for "Eleanor" on our trip across France. The French had chalked their names and town names on her hull, on her cat's eye lights we had hung some German helmets, and all over was our gear; musette bags, sleeping bags, canvas covers, and so on. The woman looked us over with distaste and then said to her companion, in English, "Look at this. How droll." We didn't say anything, and they walked slowly back to their castle. We felt like making them hurry with a few well-placed .50 caliber shots near their heels, but of course we didn't. They certainly were far from typical of the French we met in the little villages.

Some days, we were "Spearhead" and rode on the back decks of the tanks of E Co. 33rd Armor that was usually moving in areas where the enemy was suspected to be waiting, or where our 3rd Armored Air Force—the little artillery spotter Piper Cubs--had spotted something out of the ordinary. If anything on the ground did prove to be bad, we were ordered off the tank and onto the ground out in front of the tank. We would scout ahead and check houses and woods for any sight of the enemy. With an "all clear", we waved the tank forward. These tank-infantry tactics, we said with half a smile, were based on the fact that the Shermans cost more money than "us dogfaces". But the reality of it all was the fact that our job was to be the eyes and ears for the tank and to protect it. We needed their heavy firepower when things got sticky.

We crossed the Seine River, the Marne River, and the Aisne, then into Soissons, a big city. All of the cities and fields where the Allied Expeditionary Forces fought in

World War One were once again objectives for our army. In Soissons, an old French gentleman showed me scars on a building. "Bullets and shrapnel made the scars," he said. "Here, the Germans in 1915, and again in 1941. Here, the Yanks in 1918" as he pointed to holes in the wall. I think he even said there were marks from the Franco-Prussian War.

(E company, 2nd Platoon crossing a pontoon bridge over the Seine River in France.)

On we rolled—stop and go. We were not roaring into towns with all guns blazing, as the newspapers at home described what Patton's outfit was doing. Tactics like that came much later at the German border and beyond when the resistance became stiffer, and we did "reconnaissance by fire." At this stage in France, we were cautious and careful, but always moving rapidly on our objectives.

We surprised many Krauts with our speed. In towns the enemy would be relaxed, thinking they were far behind the lines, not expecting us to show up for days, even though they knew we were coming for them. Then suddenly there we were, while they were sitting and having a glass of wine. Abruptly, they were prisoners of war.

Other groups started to run and were shot at, usually with small arms. There was no use wasting a cannon shell on a guy on a motorcycle.

When our Combat Command B column slowed and stopped, we would disembark and relieve ourselves by the road, then eat, sleep, or just sit around waiting. If we were waiting for a bridge to be built, the wait could be most of the day. No roaring tanks with guns blazing in this part of the war. It was boring as hell, but still a good way to fight a war! Naturally, at our level no one told us why we stopped. The war could have been cancelled for all we knew.

One stop was a bit dramatic. We were up near the head of the column. Our tracks of the 1st Platoon were mixed in with the 1st Platoon 33rd tanks. The forward tanks caught a truck at the crossroads ahead of us and blew it apart. They also machine-gunned some Krauts on the ground.

We were alert and ready on Eleanor when another truck came barreling over the road on our left, going toward the crossroad. Our second tank turned his turret and put a shell into the radiator, burning the truck. While it was burning, I heard the snap of a bullet nearby. We looked around but couldn't see anything. When another crack was heard, I told Steve Serbin who was on the left .30 caliber machine gun (MG) to put some tracers into a haystack out in the field to our left. As he did, I fired our .50 caliber MG at the stack and we soon had it burning. There might not have been any Kraut snipers in the stack, but we took no chances.

Two of the tanks and a half-track were sent off to make a recon on a side road, but we sat where we were.

I took one of the men and we walked over to look at the German truck that had stopped burning. It was a black mess. Looking into the cab, I saw a large pocketknife in a big pile of black/gray ash. I started to reach for it, and then realized what I was looking at. The knife was in the burned pocket of the burned driver. He was not recognizable as a man, just a blackened mass. I didn't take the knife.

We walked back to the crossroads and saw another horror. One of the Germans that had been killed had been laying in the road. When the tanks came back from the Recon, they ran over one of the men. He became part of the road, absolutely flat.

Later one of our tank dozers came up. These are Shermans with a big bulldozer blade mounted in front. This tank dozer pushed the burned truck and all the bodies into the ditch to clear the road.

We went back to our track. I was up in the .50 caliber MG ring mount, just waiting. I watched some of the tankers go out to the truck where I saw the pocketknife. They pried the driver out of the cab, took him to the side of the road, and buried what was left of him. They put up a cross over the grave; it was crude and rough, but still a cross.

CC B moved on to the city of Laon and through it with crowds cheering and waving. Even out in the open country, the farmers would be assembled at the side of the road to greet us.

Back at the start of our "tour" the presence of crowds along the road would embarrass us if we had to pee. But slowly we realized that the French had different habits. Men would stand by the road waving to us with one hand and peeing with the other hand. (Of course, they did turn away from the road.) We eventually caught their spirit of freedom and we relieved ourselves whether there was a crowd of French people watching us or not.

Relations within our little squad were good. We were not a warm family by any means, but we were a good solid unit. There were no bad feelings or squabbles. The men kidded each other and called each other obscene names, but we all got along well.

Sometimes it came as a start, to me anyway, that I had lived a very different life not so long ago. Suddenly I would remember my mother, father, and two brothers. They would be out of my thoughts completely for days on end, and then my mind would snap back to the States and wonder how they were, and what they were doing.

I knew that my Mother would be quietly worrying about my brother, Martin, and me. Martin was in the Air Corps, training to be a pilot. She knew I was in danger, and Martin would be following soon. Of course, she started worrying when we both were called up. She knew what our father had endured in the 9th Argyle and Sutherland Highlanders in France in 1914-15.

My father, I'm sure, was working night and day repairing the ships of Britain that came into New York Harbor. He knew the troops in Europe needed the food and ammunition that the merchant ships carried.

Billy, my younger brother, was still in grade school and growing like a weed. He was going to be the tallest one in the family. His hair was red, like dad's.

It was an unsettling feeling to suddenly think of the past and the fact that I had a real family back in another world. In the squad we were absolutely concentrated on the little world of our half-track, Eleanor. This was our universe. Little thought was given to anything outside E-12 that did not involve our survival. We lived in constant danger and were aware of that and not much else. Our connection to home and family became fainter as we chased the enemy across France.

CHAPTER SEVEN
Belgium Liege and Eupen

The column was rolling toward the East when we were told that orders were sent down from First Army HQ to change direction and to make a ninety degree turn to the North. We were to head toward Mons, Belgium. We also learned that thousands of German troops were streaming towards Germany, and we were designated to intercept them. These were the broken, but still dangerous, divisions that had been in the Falaise area, but were trying to get back to Germany. Our Division was far ahead of these enemy forces and south of their position. We were also much faster, because the bulk of the German means of transport was horse-drawn. They did not have the number of trucks and other wheeled vehicles that our First Army fielded. In addition, they could only travel by night due to the harassing attacks of the U.S. Air Corps.

At nearly all times during the day, our 9th Air Force was winging overhead waiting for us to give them a target. There were P-47 Thunderbolts, P-51 Mustangs, and some P-38 Lightnings, and we were happy they were on our side. Forward observers from the Air Corps, who traveled with our tanks, controlled them by calling in targets.

The German columns were traveling in a northerly direction, and so were we when we made our turn. Combat Command B was on the left, Combat Command A on the right, and even further to the right was our 36th in a separate Combat Command. The Big Red One—the U.S. 1st Division was also along for the ride.

As we rolled toward Mons, we crossed the Belgian border and got a greeting from the Germans; V-1 "Buzz Bombs" sputtering over our heads, apparently on the way to Antwerp or England. These were pilotless flying bombs that flew at low altitudes toward their targets until their fuel ran out, then fell to the ground and blew up. Loaded with one thousand pounds of explosives, these bombs caused thousands of casualties in London. Thankfully, none of them dropped near us, but I saw more of them later when I was rejoining the Division.

The roadside signposts told us that we were getting close to Mons, and I knew we were in the outskirts of the city when I saw tall piles of coal slag from the mines outlined against the sky. I can remember my father talking about the coal piles he saw when he fought in the first Battle of Mons in 1915 with the 9th Argyles in the British Army. In a letter home, I said I was in amongst tall coal piles and he knew where I was. The mention got past the censors since I couldn't write the name Mons, only "somewhere in Belgium."

The three combat commands set up roadblocks and wondered what would happen next. What happened was that the German columns, traveling parallel to our Division, suddenly made a right turn to bypass Mons on their way to Germany. There were 40,000 soldiers in the German formation, and only 12,000 of our troops. Working with us, though, was the 1st Division and the 9th, which were following our tracks and got into the fight.

The battle was a huge debacle for the Krauts. We captured eight thousand and the 1st Div. bagged seventeen thousand more. How many were killed we didn't know, but the final toll must have been in the thousands.

My squad was doing a sort of roving patrol, going from one hot spot to another and helping with prisoners where we could. One radio call came in for us to rush to a house on a map location to eliminate a crowd of Germans who were in the house. Halfway there, we were recalled by radio—no reason given.

There were so many prisoners that the Belgian *Witte Brigade*, an underground group, was used to herd them into fields and pen them up. Three German generals were part of the bag.

The battle was big, important, and brief. For us, it only lasted a day and a half, but we eliminated thousands of German troops that might have been employed in the bunkers of the Siegfried Line. As a result, when we hit those fortifications later, many of the front-line pillboxes and bunkers were not manned.

The 3rd Armored left the scene to the 1st and the 9th Divisions. These great outfits mopped up the remainder of the German troops, killing and capturing many thousands. Our job was to continue to spearhead the First Army on its way to invade Germany.

In CC B again, we rolled toward Charleroi, a large Belgian town. We were at the front of the column with the 33rd Armored and we had very slow going. Not from enemy resistance, but from the thousands of happy and joyful Belgians. They crowded the streets, waving their arms and flags and offering us wine and flowers. They climbed onto our vehicles when we stopped in the streets and wanted to touch us. Again, they wrote their names and "Charleroi" in chalk on the sides of our tanks and tracks. We felt like conquering heroes even though we didn't look the part. We were dirty, unshaven, and smelly—but happy.

Out of town, our next objective was Namur, a river town, so we anticipated another blown bridge. To try to get there before that happened, we rushed along the roads as fast as possible. The terrain, however, was not like the open wide plains of Northern France, where we could race at times up to 40 mph. Here, there were hills and valleys with narrow roads winding in between. We had to slow down at each blind curve and check out what was around the bend. The tankers finally got to appreciate us Dogfaces when they asked us to go ahead, on foot, to reconnoiter the area beyond their sight.

Back in Normandy, everybody did "on the job" training in Infantry Tank Tactics, where the infantry checked out a field on the other side of a hedgerow before the tank ventured forward. Before that, if the tankers sensed trouble, they put the tank in reverse and ran. Those that didn't usually took a German 88mm shell to the hull. We infantry needed the tank for its big cannon and machine guns, and the tankers needed us for protection from German Panzerfaust (bazookas) and tanks.

Somewhere in Belgium, our lead tanks went out ahead of us and got into trouble. We had dismounted and were standing on a road when the tank platoon took off without us. They rolled away about three hundred yards along a road with big trees on the left and a sloping hill going down to the right. At a bend in the road there was a crash and a bright flash, and a lot of smoke—the tanks stopped.

A tank officer yelled to us and waved to us to come forward. We strolled up and I said "Yes, Sir?"

He said, "A Panzerfaust got the lead tank. The Krauts must be in the trees down to the right. See if there is something you can do, Sarge." Again, I said, "Yes, Sir."

I gathered the squad behind the last Sherman with all the tankers watching me. I told the men, "We're going down the slope in a column, with the BAR in the middle. When I give the signal, we'll stop and turn left. Then we'll go forward toward the tree and brush line. When I think we're close enough, we'll stop, and the BAR will open up." (I can't remember who my BAR man was. I don't think it was Wes Pitzer yet; I think he joined us near Liege.) I went on, "We are not going to go into the woods if I can help it—we'll do our 'reconnaissance' by fire."

We went down the slope, turned left, and went forward about ten feet. I told them to stop and told the BAR to spray the woods. One long burst into the trees produced two Germans with their hands in the air. I motioned for them to go up to the road where the tanks were. Then I saw one of them had a pistol at his belt. I shouted to my man up at the road, "Get that pistol, it's mine." I didn't want any tanker to grab it.

The one crippled tank was abandoned to the tank rescue group, and the rest of us went forward.

When we approached Namur, my squad was riding on one of the lead tanks, and I could hear the tank's radio talk. The 83rd Recon Battalion was up ahead and said the big bridge was "blown but partially intact," which meant a big delay until the Engineers could throw a pontoon bridge across the river to get everyone over as fast as possible. We were dismounting from the tank to go back to E-12 when a lone German soldier suddenly popped out from behind a big tree and started to run. Someone to our left fired, then every small arms weapon on the tanks opened up on the poor Kraut, but everyone missed. He ran like hell through the trees (and I joked years later that he is probably still running!). Someone suggested the Division engage in some serious target practice on the rifle range. My squad didn't fire; we just watched in amazement, and secretly, some of us were rooting for the Kraut infantryman.

(36th Armored Infantry marching through Namur, Belgium)

After crossing the bridge, we were given Huy as our objective. We were in our track and rolling again along the twisty roads. Somewhere along those roads we had two bizarre episodes, one during the day and one at night. They both involved German troops who were struggling to travel east, to get home in Germany. They must have infiltrated past our roadblocks at Mons, and were now traveling when they could, to avoid us and our air force.

The first event was in the middle of the day, as we slowly made our way around a steep hill. The hill went up to our left and dropped away on our right. The column stopped, and I looked over the edge of the road from where I was in the .50 caliber machine gun ring mount. I saw some vehicles on a road below us—about 150 feet down. Then I saw that they were all gray with black crosses on their sides. I said, "Krauts down below us." All my men jumped up and went out the rear door with their rifles ready. I briefly debated with myself, then I looked at Charles Vories and he nodded. I unclamped the .50 caliber, swung it around, charged it and tilted it down.

Then I took aim on one of the German vehicles and started firing. Krauts jumped out of the trucks and scattered in all directions. They probably thought airplanes were attacking them as the bullets came through their roof panels. The first truck started to burn, so I shifted to another one. My squad was firing over the edge at individual targets.

I heard shouting and looked up from the gun. The 1st Sgt., George Savinski, was shouting up at me. "What the hell are you doing?" I told him, "Shooting at Krauts."

(Savinski had taken Sgt. Eubanks' place, and he was not liked at all. It was nothing bad that he did, he was just not a good leader.)

Savinski said "Let me up there!" so I jumped out of the ring mount and he climbed in behind the gun and fired a few wild bursts.

Just then the Lt.'s runner, Cpl. Greene, came down the road shouting, "We're moving! We're moving!" Savinski climbed down with the attitude of "that's how to do it, men." We stood silently as he ran up to the lead track. After he was gone, I said to my men "Those Krauts were lucky. He damn near hit them."

We all got back on board, started rolling, and didn't even look down to see how the Krauts were doing.

To this day, Mons has a big parade each year in September called "Tanks in Town". The parade includes of a column of antique American tanks, half-tracks, and jeeps; with the markings of the 3rd Armored Division—the liberators of Mons.

The second event was more nerve wracking to me. We had been slowly moving through the hills as daylight faded. There were no fields to coil up in, so we knew we would probably just stop right on the road to hold our position or keep on going in the dark, either of which was dangerous. There were straggling Germans still all around us, and we could get hit by an ambush.

The decision came back that we were holding position.

We stopped. There were some tanks just behind us—about two half-tracks back, as we spaced ourselves along the road.

It was getting really dark, and I started to get nervous about the hill that rose from the road to our right. It was steep, but short, and I thought, "What if there are enemy troops up there ready to pounce on us like we caught them - when was it, yesterday?"

I told my men that I was going up to take a look. I slung my rifle and started up, holding on to branches and roots as I climbed. Near the top, I heard voices coming from the field above me. I stopped. The voices were German; I didn't understand what they were saying.

Then I heard another voice down below. It was one of the tankers walking down the road, and he had seen my movement up in the bushes. He said in a loud voice, "Hey, what's going on up there?" I heard him cock his pistol, the usual .45 side arm. I couldn't answer him—the Germans would hear me. Then luckily, I heard my men run over to shut him up and I waited a bit longer right where I was; then I heard the Germans moving off. I climbed down, half ready to shoot the tanker, but he was gone too.

CHAPTER EIGHT
In the Moonlight

The next day, our task force crossed one of the bridges at Huy, then turned left along the river. Up ahead was a huge old fortress dominating the valley. The column stopped just below the building when some resistance developed ahead. We sat in the hot sun, had some K rations, and waited—bored and tired. A couple of us decided to go up to look at the fort and as we got closer, it loomed over our heads. There was a large arch with a big wooden door studded with iron and a smaller door within the big one. I said, "What the hell" and knocked on the little door with my rifle butt. We heard some noise, then the door opened, and an old man looked out. He stared at us and we stared back. Then he said, "American?" and we said "Yes." He bowed low and said in good English, "It is yours" as he swung his arm toward the fort. We laughed and said, "No thanks" and shook his hand. We let him be and walked back to the half-track.

The rest of the squad was still taking things easy. It was a stop-and-go war. They were writing letters, reading old ones, sleeping or just sitting and talking. I opened a K ration and sat down by the roadside. I mentioned these rations before, so maybe it's time I described what they were in detail.

Actually, we had two types of rations. There were the C and the K types, and the C rations came in two cans, M (meat) and B (bread). The M unit of the C ration had varied meat and vegetables. The B unit had candy, toilet paper, biscuit, coffee and sugar, cigarettes and matches. These were all pretty good, but they were heavy to carry.

The K ration was lighter. The full day's ration consisted of three boxes. The breakfast box was a small can of egg product, dinner was a can of cheese product, and supper was a meat product. Cigarettes, chewing gum, matches, toilet paper, candy, biscuits, and instant coffee or lemonade was included in the boxes. These three rations were supposed to keep us going for one day.

There were other rations that we rarely saw. Those were the 10-in-1s, designed to feed ten men for one day. These rations had a good variety of items like cereal, jam, canned milk, canned fruit, and chewing gum. For some reason, the 10-in-1s went to HQ people and tankers. Of course, we requisitioned (stole) them whenever we saw them in the back of a truck or tank.

There was also the D bar, which was provided for emergency use. It was made of strong, black chocolate and allegedly packed with vitamins or something. We avoided them. Shaving the bar with your knife was the only way to get bits to chew. It was hard as a brick; you couldn't bite into it.

Soon we were on the way again. This time we were going to take Liège, a very large city. The plan was for CC A to go straight at the city in a frontal assault, while we in CC B swung around to the south to stop the enemy as they retreated.

Our Task Force Lovelady was assigned a roadblock at the edge of Fléron, a suburb. There were some small houses at a T-intersection in the road, facing onto wide fields, which were in front of our position. Our half-track went into a garage behind the roadblock, and we went out to the foremost of the houses. A tank settled down on our right. My squad was in a house to the left, behind a small stone wall. We waited. I set guard as the sun went low in the sky.

I was reading off the times for guard duty when one of the men said "Hey, look at this."

A platoon of Germans was coming along the road toward us—on bicycles. They pedaled steadily towards us in a column of twos, and obviously didn't see us. I thought it would be great to capture the whole platoon at once.

I got ready to shout "Halt" when someone on the tank fired a shot. Then the bow gunner on the tank opened up, followed by their turret machine gun. Then my men started to fire while I was screaming, "Cease fire! Cease fire!" The firing finally stopped, and I was still yelling at the tanker and my own men. We could have captured the lot and sent them back for questioning, and we'd be ready for more. As it was, nearly all of the Germans escaped, pedaling madly back the way they came. It was the worst mass shooting I'd seen since the episode back at Namur. Hundreds of rounds had been fired and there were only three bodies lying out in front of us. What lousy shooting!!

Darkness fell, and I put on a one-man guard with the rest inside the house. Civilians were still in there, and they welcomed us. We shared our rations, and had fun watching their wonder at our pre-packaged foods.

Checking on our guard, I heard moaning out in front of our position. One of the Germans was wounded. He called "hilf—hilf" but we didn't dare go out in the dark to help him. Then my turn came for guard, about three in the morning; he was still groaning and calling.

There must have been a moon that night, because I could see objects out in the fields. I was looking at some bushes and trees to our left front when I suddenly saw a squad of Germans approaching. I could see their rifles, helmets, and packs clearly and distinctly in the half-light. I could hear their equipment rattling. I wanted to shoot, or fire three times to warn the squad. Then I thought I'd just start firing at them as they moved away from the brush line. I looked down at my rifle briefly as I snapped off the safety, and then looked up to pick a target.

They were gone! Impossibly, the whole German squad that I had seen had disappeared. I stared and searched, then rubbed my eyes and searched again. The bushes and trees were there, but no Germans.

Then I realized that I'd been hallucinating. They were never there. I was seeing things! Fatigue, stress, fear, and exhaustion were taking their toll.

At first light everyone was on alert. We looked down the road, and saw the three bodies, and ten or eleven bicycles lying on the road. I got angry again when I remembered all those enemy soldiers riding and running for the horizon. What a waste of ammunition.

One of the new replacements didn't move fast enough when I told him to do something, and I growled at him. He was actually a good soldier, but I was still mad.

I decided to go and check on the Germans and walked out in front of the roadblock. The bodies were about seventy feet away, near the side of the road. I didn't expect to see any of them alive. Two were dead, but the third one had his eyes open and he was looking at me. His face had a greenish-yellow pallor. His legs were entangled in the spokes of the bike, and one of his legs was bloody. I pulled a blanket from one of the packs that was lying there and covered him. He said something in German, then he moved, and his arm came out from under him and it held an automatic pistol. I snapped off the safety on my rifle, but all he did was hand his weapon to me, which I took. Neither of us said anything.

I started to turn to shout for a medic when I heard a roaring engine sound. It was coming from the enemy side of the roadblock. I didn't wait; I ran across the road toward the brush line and went out into the tall grass and hit the dirt. I heard the engine getting closer and at first, I thought it was a tank. But there wasn't any rattling of treads, and it was coming too fast for a tank.

Gunfire started from the roadblock and bullets started snapping and cracking all around me. I was as flat as I could get, but I could hear the grass and shrubs being cut just above me. I screamed and yelled and swore, but the firing kept up for a few more minutes, then slowed, and stopped. I was afraid to stick my head up, but I slowly got my feet under me and started to rise. I was in a crouched position, moving up, when I heard running steps. I looked out above the grass and saw a German officer running across my right front. I rose higher as he stopped and looked back toward our tank and the roadblock. In his right hand he had a pistol, and then started to turn towards me. I did not hesitate or raise my rifle but fired from the hip then dropped back into the grass. Hearing voices, I looked up and saw my squad coming across the field. I shouted, "Over here!" and stood up. We walked toward the German who was lying on his back. He was dead. I had hit him just over his left pocket. His pistol was still in his hand, and I took that and the holster. It was a beautiful P38. I looked inside his officer's cap and saw that his name was Helm. I think his first name was Konrad, and he was a lieutenant.

We went back to the roadblock, and I saw what had happened. A German open touring car had tried to run the blockade and was now sitting in the road in front of the tank. In the car were a dead general and his driver. I got his aide, I figured.

Things were hectic after that. People were coming from everywhere. It seemed the general was General Konrad Heinrich, the head of the 89th Infantry Division, an important enemy. One of our officers came by and I stopped him and told him, "I've got another one out there in the field."

The general was taken from the backseat of the car and placed on a raised platform. His driver aide, a major, was placed on a lower platform, and the lieutenant I hit was on the ground. Rank, even in death, has its privileges. The men from the Signal Corps arrived, and pictures were taken of the bodies, not of us Dogfaces.

We didn't see the end of the day's events—it was still early morning because we were alerted to get moving again. We took our gear and walked back to where Eleanor, old E-12, was in the garage. T/5, Charley Vories, had her all gassed up.

I don't remember what happened, but we didn't move when the word came. Maybe I was talking to the squad about something. Sgt. Cofer came roaring into the garage and tore into me for delaying the column and stopping the war. He stalked off with his Tommy gun and the distinctive bullet holes in his helmet.

We rolled out into the road again, headed east. When we were back at the roadblock in Liège, civilians came and went around us. They would bicycle past or stop and talk. I asked one of them, an elderly man, to tell me the next town to the east. He said, "Aix-la-Chapelle". I nodded, not knowing he was using the old French name for Aachen in Germany. I didn't understand yet how close we were to the German border.

Vories said he had a full tank of gasoline, but we heard that the whole Division was running low on fuel. The petrol supply line extended all the way back to Normandy, and we were out at the far end. Rumors then circulated that some of Patton's people had raided one of the 3rd Armored Division's petrol dumps at gunpoint and had stolen several truckloads of gas. Patton supposedly had clapped and laughed when he was told about it. In our minds, we then began to lump him in with the Krauts.

(Photos, previous page, top: A girl throws roses to American soldiers on a 33ʳᵈ Armored tank as it enters Liege, Belgium. Previous page, bottom: Liege, Belgium, 1944. This page, U.S. tank firing its machine gun at a German sniper in Liege Belgium.)

CHAPTER NINE
All the Luck

Task Force Lovelady pushed on toward the east and met more and more resistance. The retreating Germans did everything to slow us down, and they only partially succeeded. Blown bridges were quickly overcome with pontoon substitutes. Felled trees were bulldozed aside or blown apart with a charge of explosives. Roadblocks of infantry and antitank guns were blown away by cannon fire, or artillery was called in. If those failed, we called the Air Force.

At one road junction we were dropped off of the tank we were riding on and asked to go forward to check a stand of trees that looked as if they were set up to be felled. I spread my men out as we went down the road and approached the trees. Each one was tall and had a necklace of explosive charges around its trunk, about four feet up from the bottom. There seemed to be no Krauts in sight, but that was normal. They had a charging device somewhere and maybe they were waiting for us to go down into the trees before they turned the handle—or maybe not. Maybe they had run when they heard our tank. Just maybe!

I didn't want to go into the ditch alongside the road

because that's where they would place anti-personnel mines. So, I told two of the men to come with me and told the rest of them to stay back to cover us. We walked down the road between the trees, following the fuse cord that laced them together. I tried not to think about the explosives within twenty feet of our heads. At the end of the line we spotted the charging device lying in the grass, abandoned by the Germans. We didn't touch it but left it for the Engineers to play with and called the tanks forward.

We climbed onto the back deck of our tank and the column went on towards a new town. This one was Verviers, still in Belgium, and we got two receptions: one from the happy Belgians, and the second in the form of shelling from the Germans. To save gas, the tanks were left at the edge of town and we doggies were sent in on foot.

Night was approaching as we got to the objective, and we were ordered to stop and hold where we were. Our position was a city street on the east side of large buildings—hard concrete and stone, no digging in here. German shells were hitting around the city, and I decided I didn't want us to be where we were. The shells were coming in from the east, so I moved the squad around to the west side and told them to sack out where we were in the street. Guard was set, and we tried to sleep on the concrete sidewalk, snuggled up against a building.

Little groups of young Belgian men were roaming the streets, singing and cheering the liberation. But we started to notice the odd fact that every time a group would dance by, shortly thereafter five or six German shells would come smashing into the area. We got suspicious that they were signaling the Germans, but decided it was probably just a coincidence.

In the morning we moved out. When we went around the corner - past our previously-assigned position - I saw that several shells had hit the street and sidewalk where we originally stopped for the night. Another squad had decided to place themselves in the same position. There was a great splash of blood up the side of the building. Some GIs sleeping against the building had taken a direct hit.

At the assembly area on the edge of Verviers we climbed on board E-12, moved out into the column and rolled east—Task Force Lovelady was on the way to Germany.

Between us and the German border, though, was the town named Eupen. This place was close to the German border and had changed hands between the Belgians and Germans during several wars. The people of Eupen had divided loyalty, which we didn't know when we approached the city. What was evident was the fact that there were no cheering crowds, no flags, nothing.

Something else was missing. We left Eleanor to ride to the Eupen outskirts on the Task Force tanks. At the edge of town our Shermans stopped, and the tankers said in effect, "Why don't you fellows go on without us? We'll join you later." They were out of gas.

We climbed down from the tank and the platoon assembled at a point up the road toward the town. Sgt. Cofer had a map of the streets. We were assuming the worst due to the lack of civilians to greet us. We had a strong feeling that the greeting would be done by the German army.

I started to worry about what we were facing because we had not taken any extra ammunition or grenades, and we were unprepared for any serious street fighting. We were hoping for the same reception we'd had in all the other French and Belgian towns. Back there we received kisses and wine. This town looked cold and forbidding, but we went forward anyway.

Once again, Sgt. Cofer nailed me for a job. He said, "Cullen, take your squad and get into the lead. The 3rd Squad will be behind you, then the 1st squad. The rest will take another route." He showed us the maps and the directions we were to take. I sent two of my men out as point, and we went into the town.

It was very quiet. We saw curtains twitch, so we knew the civilians were watching us as we slowly made our way through the streets. Now we knew that there must be German troops nearby. These people didn't fear us, they feared the fight that was about to happen. When my point men slowed down, I waved them on and they passed a big church. When I got up there I heard a shout behind me. Our 3rd Squad Leader, Sgt. Stan Rich, shouted,

"Jim, I'm going to take a look up here," and he pointed to an alley on the left of the street. He took part of his squad and went into the alley.

I turned back to our route and there was a single shot. It came from the alley, so I ran back and saw Stan being dragged out by two of his men. He had been shot in both legs. The single bullet had gone through his legs from the side. He was bleeding badly and was lying face down on the sidewalk, in a small, paved square protected from the alley by buildings. The men tried to stop the bleeding while we yelled for a medic. I started to ask Stan what had happened when he reached inside his field jacket and took out a small camera.

He said, "Here, Jim. I guess I've been carrying this camera just for this. Take my picture."

I took two pictures, and then I heard shouting and swearing coming from the alley. Sixty years later I would learn through correspondence with Anne-Marie Noel-Simon, a Belgian historian, what had happened. A German rear guard unit had set up an anti-tank gun to try to stop us. An officer with a pistol was directing the Krauts when Stan and his squad surprised them. The officer shot at Stan and hit him in the legs. The Germans then ran.

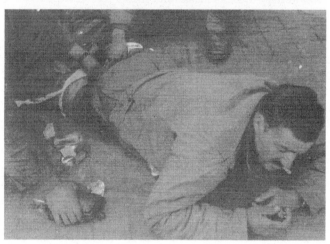

(Photos, top and center: the photos James K. Cullen took of
Stan Rich in the alley as he is being attended by medics for a
single shot through both legs. T/Sgt. Jim Cofer is glaring at
Cullen from the left in the top photo. Bottom: The same alley in
Eupen, Belgium today.)

The shouts from the alley got louder, and then an M1
went off. At the sound of the rifle shot, I ran into the alley.
On the ground was a civilian, but he was wearing some
kind of uniform jacket. He was flat on his back, and his
feet were drumming on the ground. One of Rich's men
had his rifle up in his arm and held a small booklet in the
other. The page was open at the identification photo and I
saw a swastika. I asked what happened and the GI said,

"He didn't answer the question right. He was a damn
sniper. We caught him running across the alley."

I looked again at the civilian, and he was very dead.
Anne-Marie-Noel-Simon also solved this mystery, when
she sent me the information about how Stan was shot. She
discovered that our "German sniper" was actually a
Belgian postman. The poor man was just in the wrong
place that day.

I left the civilian in the alley and went back to the street where Stan lay on the cobblestones in the little square. The medics had arrived and had taken Stan away. Cofer was also there and he said, "hold your position." We sat on the steps of the church across the street and waited. Some doors across the street opened, and two women came out with buckets of water. We watched in silence as they washed Stan Rich's blood from the sidewalk. They didn't look at us or greet us. Then a tall, heavy man came down the street past the church. He had a large pitcher in his hands and some cups. Stopping where my men were sprawled on the church steps, he offered them a drink. I said, "Watch it. What is he giving you?" They looked and sniffed, then smiled. "It's beer—heavy beer." Some of them had a cup of beer, and the man took the empties, turned and went back up the street. There was not a word or a smile from him. Some of the women came out again, went into the alley, looked at the dead civilian, and went back into their homes. We waited.

Sgt. Cofer came up the street as I was about to go to sleep and said, "OK, everybody up. We got the wrong road and we are going back. Just reverse the order. 1st squad will take the lead, then 3rd, and you guys."

In effect, we changed direction by doing an about face, and we held up the rear. Our route took us down a street then a right turn. As we came around the corner, I saw that we had a single Sherman with us. The tank slowly crawled over the sidewalk of the street toward an open area. There seemed to be a small park at the opening.

From where we were at the rear, I watched the lieutenant's runner, a fellow named Greene, walk past the tank, then stop and point toward the front. As he did this, there was a sharp explosion, and Greene's upper body rose into the air, his rifle in his hand, and his helmet still on his head. His lower body and legs flew across the front of the tank. The anti-tank shell that had hit him then smashed into the wall of the building around the corner and took out three more men. Their buddies dragged them back into the street where we stood, helpless. The wounded men were dripping blood from many shrapnel hits.

Our Sherman then fired on the anti-tank gun and put it out of action. There was a lot of shouting and yelling for medics, then we got the signal to get out of there, which we did. We retraced our steps back to our track and waited for orders.

We talked about the fact that we had found the war again. We all wondered what the days ahead would bring. The German border wasn't far away, and our Task Force Lovelady was headed straight toward it. Well, maybe not in a straight line, because the German army wanted to stop us from invading their Fatherland. We also talked about the luck we had back in the street. If we hadn't been sent in the wrong direction, we would have been in the lead when the anti-tank gun hit our people. We started thinking that we were a lucky squad, and knew we could use all the luck we could get.

CHAPTER TEN
Siegfried Line

The squad was assigned to a tank near the head of the line when the column moved out. Hills and narrow roads slowed us up as we moved forward toward the Belgium-Germany border. We had all heard of the vaunted "Siegfried Line" and read about it in the newspapers. The Germans bragged about the deadly fortifications with interlaced crossfire from machine guns and cannon. Pillboxes were supposed to be artfully hidden and disguised as innocent farmhouses. It was bad enough knowing the Germans were getting ready for us, but what made it worse was knowing they would be fighting from fortresses and we would be on foot.

Approaching a small town close to the border, our Task Force saw that there were no welcome mats out for us, so every vehicle slowed down. We scanned all the houses on the road but couldn't see anything suspicious. However, there were no flags, no civilians, not even a dog to greet us. My squad, on the lead tank, was ordered to check the road as we came to a "T" intersection, with buildings on both sides.

Climbing down from the tank, we started forward towards the end of the street. Just as we passed the front of the tank's hull, the tanker fired his main gun—the 75mm. The muzzle blast blew my helmet from my head. Some of my men were sprawled on the ground with me. After I got up, I pounded my rifle butt on the side of the tank and called them every name I could think of. The tank commander didn't apologize. He said he thought he had seen something on the hill up ahead. I told him again that he was a stupid SOB, and he confirmed my opinion in the next few minutes.

I took my squad up to the T in the road. There was a store at the corner, and I looked around to the right. Coming down the road toward us was a German assault gun—an ugly monster with a low-slung main gun. I waved to our tank and indicated a target to the right. He rolled up to the corner and stuck his gun around and fired—before we could get out of the area. The store had a large plate glass window, and it exploded and showered down on me and four of my men. I looked for blood on all of us, but saw none, not a scratch.

The German was burning when we looked again, and once more I hit the tank with my rifle and swore at him, not that either bothered the tankers. We loved the tanks at times, but they also were a pain in the ass. They were noisy, and that noise attracted enemy fire. They also created dust, and that became an artillery target.

The column moved on. More felled trees held us up slightly but didn't stop us.

The border crossing was at the little town of Roetgen. Our group was waiting in the woods for marching orders when we heard that Col. Lovelady had sent a tank unit that had gotten stuck in the mud just short of crossing the line into Germany. Col. Lovelady had no intention of stopping this side of the German border.

The Colonel ordered a new mission to get moving, "Reconnaissance in Force", The Reconnaissance Co. of the 33rd Armor, and we were in the middle of it. As we assembled I saw what a Reconnaissance in Force meant.

There were two jeeps and two Greyhounds (six-wheeled cars with a thirty-seven MM canon in a turret--it was the favorite vehicle of the 83rd Recon Company) then we had our infantry half-tracks followed by three tanks and an Engineer's half-track.

We got the go-ahead and crossed the border with the 83rd Recon leading. Task Force Lovelady, we learned, was the first unit of any army to invade Germany since Napoleon. All of us, tankers and infantry alike, jumped down at the first stop and peed on German soil.

As we passed through the town, not one German came out to say hello, but they had a lot of white sheets hanging from their windows, indicating their surrender.

On the other side at the outskirts of Roetgen, the 83rd started rapidly rolling down the road and the column moved into open country. The column moved toward the first obstacles on our path inside Germany. From my half-track I could see trouble ahead as the Recon Team stopped. There were concrete dragon's teeth on both sides of the road, and a steel gate in the middle. We were not going to get through that mess.

Our E Co. squads all dismounted and were given orders to move into the fields to protect the engineers when they moved up to the obstacles.

We formed a line abreast and started across the fields. As we approached the dragons' teeth we started to receive fire from the woods and then from concealed pill boxes.

Shouts for "Medic" started as the firing increased. It must have been about then that word passed along the line that Lt. Hall had been hit.

My squad and I were OK--we had some good cover, but we could not get up and move forward. All of E Co. was pinned down.

Later I learned that D Co. on the other side of the road was getting the same beating.

Word came up to us that Lovelady was moving up an element of the 391st Artillery and we should stay close to the ground. Shortly we heard the swishing sound of the shells as they passed over our heads and exploded to our front. The barrage lasted 5 - 10 minutes, then all was quiet in front of us.

We started forward in a new attack. Our whole line went about fifty yards and Kraut fire started cracking around our heads. Most of it was coming from one pillbox--the snipers in the woods seemed to have left the scene. Our attack stopped and the men in our squad spent the night stretched out near the dragons' teeth. It was early September. The air was warm, and we had good protective cover from any shots the Krauts might fire out at random. We didn't even dig in as we were too tired and worn out.

At first light we were ordered to attack again. This time two of our tanks had moved up the road and started firing with their bow machine guns and their canon and then aimed a few shells at the aperture of the pill box to try and quiet the Jerrys down.

To our left, one of the platoons' squads found a small ravine and one man at a time crawled forward and managed to get to the right side of the concrete pill box. My squad followed them, and I sent my squad around them to the opposite side. Now we had them surrounded.

We started yelling at the Krauts to come out "Comme Raous" and "Hande Hoch" "Come Out!"

The tank shells and our shouting must have convinced them because the pill box door opened, and twelve Krauts came out with their hands in the air and we searched them for any weapons. We then guided them down the hill to be picked up later by the MPs.

On the right side of the road, D Co. had the same success and the engineers' half-track came up on the line and then blew up the steel gate with TNT. A tank dozer filled in the hole in the road where the blown bridge was.

With that we re-assembled on the road, ate some K rations and slept in Eleanor until we got orders to move on into Germany. Unfortunately, we hadn't gotten all the snipers. On the road we got word that Lt. Hall was dead. Hearing that, we all agreed that his brown leather jacket must have made a good target for the sniper. The Jerry snipers loved to see any indication that the soldier was an officer. They delighted on seeing a gold bar on the shoulder or a leather jacket. All the rest of us had on light tan field jackets. I learned later Lt, Hall had been hit by a single bullet.

Our Lt. Verna McCord took over the Company. At first light we were ready for a rough day. So far, the Siegfried Line was fulfilling our worries and fears.

After we got past a blown bridge and more steel beams, we made slow progress, some on foot and some in the half-track. We came off the road at one point and were told to coil up. The 83rd Recon didn't like what they sensed was ahead in a wide field. The platoon followed orders, and we stopped in position.

I was up in the ring mount and the squad was climbing out the rear door when there was a God-awful crack, and Pfc. Steve Serbin, still at the .30 caliber MG, fell over. I saw this from the corner of my eye and thought one of the men had accidentally discharged his rifle while getting out and had hit Steve. I yelled at the men, "Who did this? What happened?" but they said they didn't do it. Then there was another crack just as loud as the first one and I knew we were under fire from something big. "Bail out!" I shouted as I went over the side.

Out on the field we were all flat and wondering where the shots were coming from. We knew it wasn't small arms fire. That was confirmed by a lot of incoming heavy cannon fire up and down our line of half-tracks.

Then I saw Sgt. Savinski running across the middle of the field. He was covered from his helmet down in blood and pink and gray matter and seemed to be running just to get away from something. I learned much later that a shell had hit the man standing next to Savinski and had blown the soldier to bits.

I thought about Steve Serbin and knew that I had to get back into the half-track to see if I could do anything for him. I wondered why he was wearing a white hat when I last saw him! Later, I realized that I was seeing Steve's skull. The shell had hit him in the head, and he had been killed instantly. As I raised myself from the ground, there was the ringing crash of a shell hitting my half-track. At the same instant I felt a blow to my chest and I was knocked back to the ground. I had been hit! I pulled my shirt open at the neck, looked down and saw blood pouring from my chest – right over my heart.

There was no great pain, only a feeling of shock and surprise. Questions flew through my mind – "Was this the end? Was I going to die in this lousy German field? How would Mom, Dad, Billy and Martin get the news? Had the shrapnel hit my heart? Was I really dying? There was a lot of my blood pouring out. Better get it stopped!"

As I started to get on my feet, I looked up at my half-track. Where I had been standing in the machine gun ring-mount was an oval hole in the armor. I realized, dimly, that I'd never seen that hole before. Next to me Earl Savage was yelling. He had been hit in the arm. I said "Let's go, Earl. Let's find a medic."

Savage and I staggered down the road toward the rear. He was bleeding from the shoulder, and the front of my shirt was covered in blood. Coming toward us was Capt. Stalling. "We're catching hell back there, Sir" I said, and kept walking until someone guided us to the aid station. It was in a ditch by the road. The medics looked at us, put on an initial dressing to stop our bleeding, and tagged us. Then an ambulance rolled up. As it did, more casualties appeared. When the medics finished their immediate task, seven or eight of us were stuffed into the meat wagon and were carried farther back to a clearing station.

With that, I was out of the action at the Siegfried Line, but I found an After-Action Report that describes these three days in great detail. It was written by a 2nd Lt. Hadsel and endorsed by Maj. William Castille, the CC B Intelligence Officer.

This report has gathered all the information from the units and gives the story of the action in total. This is the picture that the GI on the ground does not see.

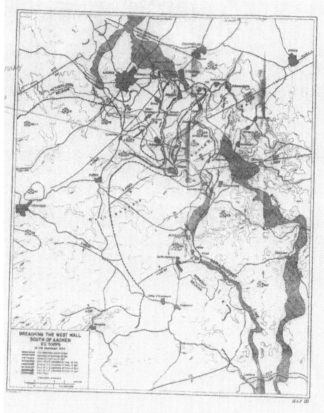

(After action report)

SIEGFRIED LINE

3rd Armored Division, Combat Command "B".

Task Force 1 (Lovelady), 12 September, to 25 September, 1944.

Interviews:
Lt. Col. Wm. B. Lovelady, C.O.
Capt. George Stalling, Ex. O.
Lt. V.L. McCord, C.O. E Company, 36th Armd Inf Regt
Lt. J.H. Haldeman, C.O. Rcn Company, 33rd Amd Regt
Lt. J. W. Wilson, 1st Plat, Rcn Company, 33rd Armd Regt

Prepared by: 2nd Lt. Fred L. Hadsel, 2nd Infoc and Hist Serv, 1st U.S. Army.

Note: This account is supplemented, both with respect to terrain descriptions and tactical action, in the accounts of the infantry, engineers, and TDs.

Composition of TF 1 (Lovelady)

Hq, 33rd Armd Regt
2nd Bn 33rd Armd Regt
2nd Bn 36th Armd Inf (-F Company)
Rcn Co. 33rd Armd Regt (-3rd platoon)
1st plat B Co, 23rd Armd Engr Bn
1st plat, B Co, 703rd TD Bn
Det. Maint Co
1 batry, 391st Armd FA (105 SP)

(Handwritten note):

Note: This report was copied by CCB from the report prepared by 2nd Lt Hadsel, and is added hereto as a supplement to the AFTER ACTION REPORT CCB for the period 12 Sept. to 25 Sept 1944

Wm. P. Castille
Major, S-2
CCB

11 Sept.

Task Force 1 (Lovelady) of CCB, 3rd Armd Division coiled for the night east of Kettenis in the fields at the edge of the Ketteniser Forest (vicinity of 815290).

12 Sept.

At 0800 Lt. Colonel Lovelady ordered Lt. Wilson, 1st Platoon, 33rd Rcn Company to reconnoiter in force a route east through the forest towards the German border. Wilson's platoon thus formed the point in a column consisting of D Company, 33rd Armd Regt, of medium tanks, and D Company, 36th Armd Inf. It proceeded northeast until it reached Baumhauershuttenschen (825295) where it turned southeast to strike unto the thick forest. The boggy ground proved too soft for the tanks, each one cutting deeper until the entire column was stuck along the trail between Baumhauershuttschen and the next cross trail (836283). Only by working some of the vehicles ahead and by dragging most of them back to the main road was Wilson able to get the unit out of the woods. Not until 1500 did the last of this reconnaissance force rejoin the column of the task force, which meanwhile had moved northeast of the cluster of hamlets, Neudorf, Botz, Pfau, and Rott (vicinity of 8531). (Note: This last village is not to be confused with another Rott around which the Task Force later fought).

When the first reconnaissance in force became bogged down, Lovelady ordered a second reconnaissance in force to proceed along the main highway in the direction of the German frontier and the town of Roetgen. This force, composed of the 2nd Plat Rcn Co, 33rd Armd Regt, E Company 36th Armd Inf and 1 plat of engineers, moved about 1130, going northeast through the cluster of hamlets Neudorf, Botz, Pfau, and Rott, and just east of Botz it took the highway southeast towards Roetgen.

Along this highway the column picked up a German machine gun crew, who surrendered without firing their weapon. The only other resistance in the western part of the forest was a lone bicycle rider, who hastily mounted his vehicle and withdrew upon seeing the column. By 1500, the reconnaissance in force had crossed the border (the time of crossing being recorded at 1451), and reached the railroad tracks in the western edge of Roetgen (903289), at which point they waited for the bulk of the task force.

The main body of the task force cleared the cluster of hamlets without incident, and with the 1st platoon of the Rcn Company now back in the lead, turned southeast on the highway towards Roetgen about 1500. The column moved at full speed down the road without flank reconnaissance. At 1620 the command group near the rear of the column crossed the border. The task force established road blocks at important junction along the highway -- one staying near the railroad tracks (903289), and another going to the southeast part of the town (920275). This latter force was originally instructed to go to the next crossroad down the highway (927270), but it hit enemy resistance and was ordered to set up its defenses nearer the town.

One battery of the 391st Armd FA picked up 12 to 15 prisoners, who had apparently been left behind to fell trees for road bocks in the Ketteniser Forest. In fact two or three road blocks of little consequence had been cleared in that area.

As the task force moved through the town of Roetgen it encountered no opposition, although a few were spotted in the southeastern outskirts which made no resistance. Holding its column formation, with the reconnaissance elements still leading, the task force turned to the left after crossing the railroad tracks (904287), and proceeded in a northeasterly direction through towards the Hauptbecken reservoir. The 2nd platoon, Rcn Company, had scouted ahead of the main body, and at 919298, just south of the reservoir, it came upon a blown bridge. At the same time, it observed the Dragons Teeth just beyond the bridge and drew fire from the pillboxes on the other side. In reconnoitering the area with the scout section, the platoon leader was killed, and the remainder of the group drew their vehicles off to the side of the road to permit the tanks of the reconnaissance in force to move forward.

The tanks, however, were bound by the road and blocked by the blown bridge. The action thereafter became one of infantry supported by tanks and artillery. The situation developed into a fire fight between 1630 and 1700.

The terrain at this point offered excellent possibilities for defense by the enemy. The highway winds up to the bridge which had been blown. Across to the right rises a steep hill, heavily wooded, on the face of which is a pillbox. The Dragons Teeth, which ran just across the bridge, extend from the hill to the left (west) up the slope of another hill, and cut a gash into the heavily wooded section in that direction. Behind the Dragons Teeth, with fields of fire dominating the bridge, the road, and the concrete obstacles. Across the gap in the teeth made by the highway is an iron gate, with three main beams, each of which has a heavy wire cable inside. As the enemy positions approached from the south, the right (east side) of the Highway offers no possibility for attack. On the left, however, the slopes of the hills give some cover through hedgerows and draws. However, the enemy fire could dominate the slopes of these hills and the bare ridges would thus be untenable.

As the column approached the blown bridge, enemy from within the pillboxes fired with machine guns, putting cross fire on the road, while mortars and small arms fire came from entrenchments near the pillboxes. No AT or artillery fire was received.

Between 1730 and 1800, the infantry moved up towards the blown bridge. As it approached it received additional sniper fire from various directions. On the left side of the road, in a series of hollow haystacks, the enemy had placed snipers, who fired on the column from the flank as it moved up. An estimated 15 to 20 snipers thus harassed the column and the company commander of E Company, 36th Armd Inf Regt, 1st Lt. A. P. HALL, was killed at this time. The 1st platoon deployed along the hillside on the left of the road, while the 2nd platoon was stretched along the slope east of the road, from a point near the blown bridge back several hundred yards to the first road junction. In view of the lateness of the hour and the nature of the enemy resistance, the infantry was ordered to consolidate for the night. The 1st platoon moved over to some houses on the left, while the 2nd platoon conducted reconnaissance in the vicinity of Roetgen itself. It then set up a road block vicinity of 903289, assisted by two tanks.

In view of the necessity of pushing forward as fast as possible, however, a change of plans was made late in the afternoon. Between 1930 and 2000, D Company, 36th Armd Inf was ordered to pass up the road to the blown bridge, using as its zone of action the right side. It was given the mission of crossing the stream east of the bridge site, and of working its way up the sharp slope to the crest of the hill south of the Hauptbecken reservoir. The purpose was to establish a position between the Dragons Teeth (in reality to flank the teeth from the east, since they ended at the hill), which would protect the engineers while they built a bridge. However, the assault got only approximately 50 feet behind the line of departure (923297), where it was stopped by the small arms and machine gun fire. The enemy had excellent fields of fire, and the infantry was pinned down.

At this point Lovelady brought a battery of the 391st Armd FA to bear on the area, which with its 105mm SP guns laid a heavy concentration on the enemy position. In spite of this fire, the enemy still was able to keep the infantry from advancing. Therefore, D Company was ordered to hold for the night. The vehicles were brought back towards Roetgen, and outposts were established. It was at this time that the outpost established in the southeast part of Roetgen met resistance.

By evening, the plan of establishing a bridgehead for the engineers was as yet unfulfilled. The infantry had suffered considerable casualties and were unable to advance. Enemy aircraft were in the area during the night; otherwise it was uneventful.

13 Sept.

At daylight the two companies of the 36th Armd Inf renewed the attack. All three platoons of E Company were on the slopes of the hill west of the road (917296) and south of the Dragons Teeth. Lt. V. L. McCord, now commanding the company, moved his 2nd platoon forward towards the obstacles. As they reached the brow of the slope, not more than 100 yards from their original position, they received fire from the pillboxes the other side of the obstacles. The one at 918299 gave the most trouble. However, one squad was able to work its way, one man at a time, forward into a draw, where it had cover from the fire. The forward squad of the 2nd platoon then got through the Dragons Teeth, and edged around to the right of the pillbox. The other two squads were ordered to follow the leading squad, and one by one the men were assembled in the vicinity of the obstacles. One column was then taken around to the left of the pillbox, in the woods, while the tanks fired some rounds of AP on the apertures. The right prong of the attack closed in from the east, while the left came in from the west, while the tanks moved up (on the south side of the obstacles) and fired on the pillbox. The sight of this proved too much for the enemy, who gave up without further fight at approximately 0800.

D Company on the right side of the road worked its way as planned to the high ground south of the reservoir (vicinity of 923297). From there it moved west towards the Dragons Teeth and the pillboxes. It captured 15 to 20 of the enemy who offered no serious resistance.

By 1000 the infantry had squeezed out the enemy resistance behind the Dragons Teeth, and the engineers moved in both to fill the bridge site and to blow the gates across the road. The engineers used a tank dozer to fill the crater (in fact, the blown bridge was itself a crater), since the stream which crossed under the road at this point was dry and no bridge was at this season necessary. Three charges of TNT were required for the gate, since the wire cable inside the beams greatly increased their strength.

The 1st platoon, reconnaissance company and the infantry began to move across the streambed at 1015, and while the vehicles began their advance north about noon. All enemy resistance immediately behind the first set of obstacles of the Siegfried Line had been silenced before this time. The reconnaissance platoon proceeded along the highway, as it wound through a heavily wooded area. E Company of the 36th Armd Inf advanced on the left, while D Company moved on the right. The column went slowly, for there were several pillboxes in the valley to the west of the road. All the men were dismounted. When a pillbox (918303) opened up on the men, a tank turned to fire directly on it from a distance of about 50 yards. It then surrendered.

About 800 yards north of the Dragons Teeth, the column hit another iron gate, but as there was no resistance in the vicinity, it was quickly blown. As the column continued the advance, it passed two AT guns (one 75mm and one 20mm) which had recently been abandoned. Ammunition and machine guns were in place around the AT guns, which the task force rendered useless by destroying the sights. Several additional pillboxes were found, but only one German, obviously a straggler, was discovered. A number of trees were felled across the road, but they only temporarily slowed up the advance north in the direction of Rott (923326). About two-thirds of the way to Rott, at 1300, a large rocket gun was found, with lots of ammunition around it.

The infantry and reconnaissance platoon continued to work their way along the road, which still cut through heavy woods. When the leading elements approached the edge of the forest southwest of Rott (920324), they saw an enemy patrol, consisting of a light machine gun, a motorcycle, and a half-dozen soldiers. It scattered as the column came in sight. One tank began to fire upon the enemy, and the others joined in. In a short while, as the fire built up from Rott itself, the column edged its way into the open fields lying south of the town. As the half-tracks of the column likewise moved into the field, the enemy opened up from the town with heavy fire. Grouped in the outskirts of the village were several light AT guns, and in the field to the left were other AT guns, while on the right was an 88mm gun. Later on at least two Tiger tanks, and two Panthers came up to assist the enemy.*

Within a few minutes, the task force lost five tanks and two half-tracks by enemy fire. At 1600, when the infantry deployed at the edge of the woods, the artillery was called in, and it laid a heavy concentration on the town. The support was excellent, and shells fell within 75 yards of the troops without serious casualties.

Early in the fire fight, elements of E Company infantry, started to move west along a path in the woods (918321), in order to approach Rott from the west. Enemy fire hit one of the half-tracks as it pulled out of the woods, and under the fire the company took to the woods.

A scout of the reconnaissance platoon sighted a movement on the left flank, and shortly thereafter it was ascertained that a Panther tank was moving in behind a rise in the ground (919326). A 76mm opened fire on the tank. Two of the 12 to 15 rounds fired penetrated the tank, and the crew abandoned it. Another tank or SP 88 revealed its well camouflaged position in Rott when it fired on one of the already disabled half-tracks. Thereupon the combined fire of the tanks at the edge of the woods knocked it out.

The artillery and tank fire brought an end to the opposition in Rott shortly after 1700. At 1730, the infantry was ordered to precede the tanks into the town, and as the foot soldiers advanced, the tanks interspersed with the men, the opposition ceased entirely. The Task Force passed through the town without resistance until it reached the central crossroad (923326), where a platoon of enemy infantry was spotted along the road to the north. A couple of shells from the tanks dispersed the enemy.

The head of the column then turned north to proceed to Mulartshuette (928344), and shortly thereafter an enemy bazooka team was sighted. Tank fire broke up the team, but it reformed on the right of the road, only to be dispersed again. In view of the groups of enemy along the zone of advance, the artillery was ordered to lay down a rolling barrage ahead of the advancing column. In this manner the attack proceeded slowly but surely towards Mulartshuette. The town itself offered no resistance, but after the column had passed through and turned northwest in the center of town, it came upon a blown bridge. (930345). A platoon was sent back to check through the town, while other infantry crossed the stream to secure an area large enough to permit the engineers to rebuild the bridge unmolested. The task force then halted for the night.

14. Sept.

During the night the infantry had outposted the bridge area successfully, and the engineers worked on the construction of the bridge. In testing the strength of the half-demolished structure, the engineers called for a light tank to try to cross, whereupon the entire bridge collapsed with the tank in the middle.

Early in the morning, in spite of the rain and fog, the task force started on the road north from Mulartshuette. Less than a thousand yards beyond the bridge, it entered the thick Kornilimuenster Forest. D Company of medium tanks 33rd Armd Regt and D Company of the 36th Armd Inf, and a scout section under Lt. Wilson of the reconnaissance company, formed the advance guard of the column. No resistance was encountered in the forest, and the force reached Venwegen without difficulty (926362). When the leading elements reached the fork in the road immediately north of Venwegen, they continued on the main route to the northwest, rather that taking the secondary road to the north (right). However, the scout section soon discovered its error, when it reached a blown viaduct, whose debris blocked the road. The section retraced its route to the fork in the road, and initiated reconnaissance up the dirt route to the right. In the meantime, at 1100, the commanding general of CCB ordered the entire force to halt at the fork north of Venwegen, since the situation of Task Force 2 (King-Mills) was not yet clear south of Schmidthof. Task Force 1 therefore coiled in the nearby fields and waited for further instructions.

Task Force 2, which was follwing up the main road from Roetgen to Kornelimuenster, was halted by enemy resistance in the vicinity of Schmidthof (901327). It was therefore ordered that a combat team from Task Force Lovelady be sent west to strike the enemy from the rear. At 1130, D Company of medium tanks, D Company of infantry, and 1st platoon 33rd reconnaissance company, moved west from the road (RJ 923366), and struck southwest to the town of Hahn (914358). In the middle of the village, the column encountered a blown bridge but no enemy resistance. Two 88mm AT guns on the hill to the north (912360) were fired upon by the tanks, but these weapons had apparently already been abandoned. The column having been stopped by the blown bridge, waited at that point for the developments of Task Force Mills fight with the enemy. By early afternoon, it was clear that Task Force Mills could proceed without undue difficulty, and it came up abreast with Task Force 1.

While the column sat in Hahn, an infantry patrol searched the high ground north of the village. It found a few enemy but the guns were unmanned. After waiting about an hour in Hahn, the column turned back to its parent organization. It found that a reconnaissance in force (1 plat of B Company medium tanks, 1 plat

CHAPTER ELEVEN
Two Armies

At the Clearing Station, we waited in one large tent until a doctor examined us, and I suppose outlined what our treatments would be. At one side, a lieutenant walked back and forth, agitated; yelling and waving his arms. He was cursing and swearing, "That God damn Lovelady. Push on! Push on! Keep going! Move up! Move!"

He didn't appear to know that anyone was near him and listening to all this. I don't know what happened to him, but it looked like a case of battle fatigue. He didn't appear to be physically wounded.

I was called into a section of the tent where a doctor examined my chest, wrote something on the medical tag attached to my shirt and said, "OK. Go out to the field. They'll pick you up soon." I lost track of Savage when later, I was taken by ambulance to a field hospital back in Belgium. I never saw Savage again.

The hospital was a little tent city, with big red crosses on the canvas, and it was a complete operating hospital. A nurse took a look at the tag on my shirt and told me to take it easy, and that I'd be operated on soon. As a "walking wounded" I could move around and explore, but it felt strange walking without my rifle. I had left it in the ditch at the company aid station.

Then I smelled food. Hamburgers! I hadn't eaten all

day, and had just one K ration the day before, so I went into the mess tent and was given a big hamburger on a bun. I knew I shouldn't eat before an operation but didn't care. It tasted terrific.

I was called into another tent that was the operating room. After preparation, they stuck my arm with Pentothol which knocked me out while they removed the piece of steel embedded in my chest.

When I woke up, I was on my way by hospital train to a big hospital in Paris, and from there to a rehab center and then back through the replacement chain to the 3rd Armored.

I had a lot of time to think during the two months I was rehabilitating. It occurred to me that there were two distinct United States Armies. My time in the U.S. Army was divided by a year and a half in the States or ZI (Zone of the Interior); then time in Europe—a short time in the United Kingdom, a long time in contact with the enemy, and (eventually, shortly before the war ended) time in the Com Z (Communications Zone).

Those segments made up two Armies that existed in WWII. The first Army was the one I knew in Ft. McClellan, Alabama. It was the army of barracks, garrisons, camps, and forts. Every waking hour was scheduled and structured and accounted for. We woke at the scheduled time to the sound of a bugle at Reveille and went to sleep with a bugle blowing Taps. In between, we trained, marched, and practiced the Manual of Arms, close - order drill, bayonet drill, dry firing drill, and on and on. Meals were in the Mess Hall with two choices: "Take it" or "Leave it." The other Mess Hall order was "Take all you want but eat all you take." Waste was frowned upon.

Discipline was demonstrated in saluting all officers on sight and using "Sir" when addressing an officer. Our uniforms were dictated by the posting of the Uniform of the Day on the bulletin board in the Orderly Room. We also had an Inclement Weather Schedule. It was,

"Raincoats will be worn."

Inspections were frequent. Barracks were examined for dust and cleanliness. Everything had to be in the proper and designated place.

Personal inspections also took place. Our uniforms, gear, and weapons were part of the routine. Also, before each monthly pay day, our bodies were inspected for venereal disease before we were paid. This was called "Short Arm Inspection." We had to line up—naked but for boots and raincoat and present our penises to the Officer of the Day. What a joy for everyone!

When we stepped ashore in Normandy, the "other Army" waited for us. This was an Army in nearly direct contrast to the Stateside Army. There were no company formations, no parades—bunching up was forbidden and dangerous. Uniforms were regular OD (Olive Drab) wool with a field jacket. No ties. Helmets were worn *at all times* (this did not need an order!).

In the rear areas there was saluting and military discipline, but closer to the front—this disappeared. We said, "Sir" but rarely, if ever, saluted. As mentioned before, the Germans targeted officers first. A salute could get an officer killed.

The only sleep discipline we observed was "first light". There was no bugle blowing Reveille, just a nudge or a shove with a rifle butt. At dawn everyone had to be up and alert and on guard.

Nightfall was another story. Guard had to be posted and rotated. Sleep, for those off guard, was usually brief but deep. There was no Taps to signal when to sleep. We slept whenever we had the chance, day or night.

Chow was not in a well-ordered mess hall. Like sleep, we ate when we had the chance, if we had the chance. Regarding the chow, instead of cooked or fried or boiled meals, we ate the boxed or canned rations we carried in our packs. Hot meals from the company kitchen were a rarity. We carried a spoon; it was the only "silverware" we needed.

In the Stateside Army, mail call was something we looked forward to every day. The company clerk would signal to fall in to formation over the PA system, and we would assemble. He called the names and we either got mail or we didn't. Telephones weren't that common in 1943-45, so we didn't call home.

In Europe, our Army still got mail—V-mail, but still no phones. The Company Clerk still handled the mail, but it was sent up to us at the front on a hit-or-miss basis. It came up to us in little bundles and was distributed along the line by hand. It was easy to tell the ZI Army from the "old timers"; the Other Army. The ZI Army's uniforms were clean and neat, the Other Army's uniforms were very dirty.

In the 3rd Armored Division, I was one of fourteen thousand, two hundred and twenty-four casualties—of that number, nine thousand, eight hundred and nine were battle casualties. The rest were accidents and illnesses, both physical and mental.

I went through the system twice; the first on the way to combat, and the second to re-enter combat. Both trips were interesting and not unpleasant. A lot has been written about the Army system and how terrible it was on the morale of the men going through it. I didn't find that. On each journey I "buddied up" with other men who appeared to be pleasant, bright, disciplined, and who were enjoying Army life. We did the normal griping and complaining; we *knew* our gripes were justified, but usually ended up doing it the "Army way" anyway.

I was hit on September 13 and reported for duty to the 36th Armored Division around November 28. The Command Post was in Eschwieler, Germany and upon arriving there, I was shocked at a number of things.

I had left the Regiment at Rott, and in the two and a half months, the front line had only advanced about thirty miles into Germany. I learned that the German resistance had been fierce every foot of the way.

Most of the replacements the company picked up before Liège had been hit at the Stolberg Corridor. Throughout the whole division, the casualties had been high. Artillery fire and machine gun fire had created most of them, where the men were helpless on the back decks of the tanks. An infantryman can survive a major barrage if he is dug in, but up on the tank he is a target.

I found my squad billeted in a two-story house at the edge of the village, and they appeared to be very comfortable. In an upper floor was a small group of intelligence men, who were with Regimental H.Q. The house still had furniture in it so most of us slept in beds, and some on the floor in sleeping bags on mattresses. I was surprised to see the furniture still there. Earlier, when I came through Aachen on the replacement route, we were assigned to a large three-story apartment house. We were sent to the third floor and told to open the windows and to throw out all the furniture. "All of it? Why?"

The replacement non-com said, "It's German, throw it out."

We followed orders and threw it out. Beds, wardrobes, trunks, dressers, and chests of drawers were all pushed to the windows and heaved into the courtyard. Quite a pile resulted. Everyone's attitude was "It's German—the Krauts deserve it."

E-12, old Eleanor, was parked beside the house. The big hole in her armor was a little rusty, but it was a battle scar. I asked Charley Vories, the driver, if he had found my musette bag. He said, "No, Sarge. When that shell came in, it went right through your bag."

"So, I guess my P-38 pistol went with it?"

"Yep. Everything disappeared."

I met the few old-timers, and the new replacements. I also met the squad leader, S/Sgt. Darrell Harbert, who had taken over the 2nd squad after I was wounded, and which now had two sergeants. The problem was solved when

Harbert was given another squad and I took over my old 2nd squad. Later Harbert was hit in the leg during the first days of the Bulge and left the regiment.

Many books recite the loneliness of the replacement in the front-line squad. They write about the poor guy joining a squad of veterans who ignore the green kid and don't gather him into the group. I'm sure this happened in some companies, and probably in the 3rd Armored too. It all depended on the Squad Leader. If he was a cold, selfish bastard, then the rest of the squad was too. I tried to make our replacements feel that we needed them and were glad to have them in our unit. We had to do that for two reasons: it was the right thing to do, and because a fearful, panicky GI could jeopardize the whole squad.

The Germans had a different system. The Wermacht withdrew a whole division from the front to rest the men, repair their equipment, and then absorb new men into the squads.

Sixty years ago, you became instant buddies if another GI asked, "Were you near Saint-Lô?" and you said "yes". This is still true today. Saint-Lô, Falaise, Mortain, Mons, and St. Vith. These were battles that happened in 1944 that formed an immediate connection. Back then, they were names that were known to just a few of us in the American Army. Now those names are in the history books, and some are on the World War II Memorial in Washington, D.C.

CHAPTER TWELVE
O' Tannenbaum

The relatively peaceful period upon my return to duty enabled me to get to know the new men in the squad, and to let them know me. The introduction I had to my first squad back in Normandy had been a quick "hello", and then immediately into combat. This time I was able to talk to the men and learn a little more about them before we went into action. We sat in our house and talked about life back in the States and wondered when we would see the U.S. again.

The talk was neither deep nor brainy. We didn't discuss the purpose of the War or how it had all started. Hitler was never mentioned, and if the name did come up, it was preceded by "that fucking..." The German soldier was talked about and he was called a variety of names; Jerry, Herman or Kraut, even Allemand, the French word. The word "Nazi" wasn't in our vocabulary.

My little replacement group stayed a day or two in these sad conditions, and then we were trucked up through the Hürtgen Forest and back to the Division.

Although we had furniture in Eschweiler, we had no German civilians. They had all been chased to the rear; not that our Division was exactly at the front. We were in reserve, deep reserve. Most days we cleaned equipment. Sometimes we read the little army issue, pocket-sized books that came with our rations and were on topics ranging from novels to jokes, to the news. Other times we wrote letters home, or reread letters from home. Some days we did house-to-house combat training in the empty village homes. We attacked the empty houses in mock combat to teach the new replacements how to get some coordination in the effort to clear a town. We showed the new men that two GIs can't go through the same doorway at the same time. Also, that it was better to throw a grenade into a suspicious room instead of sticking your head around the corner. Grenades were expendable, heads were not.

I told the squad about an episode that had happened back in France. We were clearing a house in a small village. Some Krauts had run when we rolled into town, but we had to be sure they were all gone. I was carrying a .45 pistol instead of my rifle because it was easier to use in house searches and I went up a ladder into the attic with my gun hand out in front. I heard one of the men say, "There's something making a noise down there in the basement." I came down the ladder and we shouted down the basement stairs in lousy French, German, and American to "come out" but we heard nothing but some mysterious soft scratching sounds. I didn't want to send anyone down into the dark basement, so I said, "Drop a grenade down there; that will get an answer."

Roy pulled the pin on a grenade, let the lever flip, and tossed it down the stairs. It exploded. Real hand grenade explosions produce nothing more than some black smoke and dust. A movie grenade always looks like a can of gasoline blowing up—all bright flame and smoke. Also, a movie grenade will always blow a house apart—not so. We were startled by the loudest screaming howl from the dark, and then the biggest police dog any of us had ever seen came flying out of the basement door and bowled past us.

If you think we frightened the dog, he scared the shit out of us!

Also, during this lull, we wandered to nearby houses and "liberated" things we liked. Looting was against U.S. Army regulations, but we weren't doing that. Some GIs picked up small wagons to take with them on their "liberating" tours. Anything that we liked, we took. We went through personal items in the homes as if we lived there and were shopping for someone's birthday. Silverware, watches, toys; anything that struck our fancy was liberated. Our consciences didn't even blink. We were "liberating" from the Germans, and they didn't count.

Christmas was coming. In the woods we found a small balsam tree and set it up in the kitchen. We had our pick of very fine Christmas ornaments and light bulbs. After all, the best Christmas decorations were made in Germany. For tinsel, we went outdoors and picked up "chaff," the aluminum strips our bombers dropped to foul up the German radar. Soon we had a beautiful tree, but it needed lights and color.

One of my men had an inspiration. The S-2 Regimental Intelligence group was about two hundred yards away, and they had a generator running night and day. "Why don't we tap into the power, then we'll have a real home here. I know how to do it Sarge. It'll be easy."

We organized a squad combat patrol and cautioned our intelligence buddies upstairs not to say anything. That evening we boldly did the deed. Wire was no problem; there were miles of it lying around the fields. We picked up a large reel of cable, and our electric expert tied into the generator while the rest of us acted as if we were on an authorized operation. I directed traffic in the road while the wire was strung over the road and connected. Back at the house, it was a simple matter to make the connection, hang blankets on the windows for blackout, and then "there was light." Our little Christmas tree lit up and we were truly joyful.

A radio was liberated and plugged in, and we gathered around it and turned it on. The first sound we heard was music! It was Bing Crosby singing "I'm Dreaming of a White Christmas." None of us said anything—we couldn't. Actually, we couldn't even look at each other; we were too filled with emotion.

The days were pleasant even though they grew colder and wetter each week. It was nearly the middle of December, and winter was coming. We walked around the fields shooting at German helmets that were lying in the ditches. We shot holes in them with German pistols.

Engineer's Mackinaw coats were issued to us as the weather got colder, and there were more and more cloudy rainy days. These were great winter coats; they came down to mid-thigh, and we could get in and out of the half-track without stepping on the bottom of the jacket. Also, climbing to the back deck of the tanks was easy, and best of all, the jackets were warm and waterproof.

One day I was looking up at a squadron of American P-51 Mustangs flying just under a cloud cover. Suddenly a single Messerschmitt Me-109 dropped from the cloud cover right into the middle of the squadron. The German pilot realized he had made a *big* mistake, rolled his plane on its back, and bailed out. His parachute floated down toward the German line. The U.S. squadron didn't even bother to pursue his plane, they stayed right on their course. The Me-109 came down like a brick and buried itself in the field.

That night we heard our anti-aircraft blasting away, and we went out to watch. Kraut planes were overhead, and they were dropping bombs. We watched the show until we heard metal chunks hitting Eleanor, our half- track. It was shrapnel from the anti-aircraft guns, so we quickly dashed inside for cover.

The night after the Kraut aircraft bombed us, our two intelligence GIs came down from the second floor. They said that they had a report at HQ-G2 that the Germans had made a counter-attack in the US lines to the south of us, in Belgium, but that news didn't worry us a bit. We had our own war up here in Germany, and "tough" for the troops in Belgium. The word in our latrines was that our Division was getting ready for a big attack across the good tank country that stretched before us. We knew Cologne was over the horizon and would be the prime objective for the 3rd Armored Division.

But Cologne would have to wait.

CHAPTER THIRTEEN
Ardennes

Trois Ponts, 3 Jan. Attack, Sterpigny-Cherain

I was called, with the other squad leaders, to the E
Company Command Post, where our Co. Commander Lt.
Verna McCord told us that the situation down in Belgium
was starting to look bad. The Krauts had broken through
on a broad front in the Ardennes forest area, and it looked
as if we might get called into the fight. We were to
consider ourselves "on alert" but with nothing to panic
about, so we didn't.

Mail came to us and we were able to send letters home.
Most of it came in a "V-Mail"; a small envelope with a
small photo print of the original letter. It had been
microfilmed and combined with thousands of other letters,
in small rolls of film, to save space on the ships. The Army
figured the troops needed food and ammo just as much as
they needed mail and made a great effort to get all of those
things to us in due time. Christmas packages had come in,
and we passed around cakes and candy while we read,
wrote letters home, and just continued being comfortable.
Our little tree sparkled with lights and color. The only
thing missing was our families.

The squad was becoming more of a family, though.

There were new men, and some "old" new men. Wes Pitzer and Roy Plummer had joined us around Liège, and they were good soldiers. Charley Vories was still my driver, and definitely a steady type. Recon and Savage were "long gone", as the Southern boys said. Savage, of course had been hit when I was, but I never found out what happened to Recon. A list of the whole squad somehow survived in one of my pockets, and I still have it. Unfortunately, the names on the list don't connect in my mind with a face or a memory now. I worked with many GIs during the time at Ft. McClellan doing cycle after cycle in basic training, but nearly all of their faces are gone from my memory.

The opposite is true, also. I can look at a picture of the squad or the trainees, and although their faces then become familiar, I don't remember the names any more.

In those days, though, the peaceful period continued to make us into a unit. Reubin Kline was a cheerful, voluble type; Vories, the driver, was good company and a talker too, and Vernon Spores from Clam Falls, Wisconsin lived up to his town name. He rarely talked; he just smiled a lot. Plummer was a religious man and a good soldier. He and Pitzer tied the squad together.

The 19th of December brought the panic we had ignored right to our doorstep. The Platoon runner knocked on our door and said we were on Three-Hour Alert. That meant that if we got the signal, then "the balloon would go up" in three hours.

But that did not happen. Instead, he came running back after an hour and said, "OK, saddle up. We're going now!" We scrambled to get our gear together, gas up Eleanor from Jerry cans, and check our ammo and rations—all the details of getting ready for combat were rushed and squeezed into action like a scene in a cartoon. Our two intelligence types from upstairs watched all this. They knew where we were going, and I heard one of them murmur, "This is just like a movie."

All of our "liberated" stuff was left behind without a

glance; we didn't need the "toys" we had picked up. We really did regret leaving our Christmas tree, though. It was a fond touch of home.

We were given our position in the company formation, and we fell into line behind E-11, "Eightball". All of our half-tracks were given a nickname by their crews that started with "E". Eleanor, Eightball, Easy Rider, etc.. The column headed south, and the situation appeared normal. As usual, we didn't know where we were going, but our objective didn't really matter to us. If the Company Commander and his staff had given us the name of a town or area, it wouldn't have meant a thing to the squad or to me, anyway. We were soldiers, and when the time came for action, we would know what to do.

Meanwhile, my men slept or just sat holding their rifles and watching the German forests roll by. Darkness put a stop to sightseeing though, and it became more and more difficult to see the cat's-eye lights of E-11 up ahead. These taillights were small and could only be seen from dead astern. An interval had to be maintained between the vehicles but losing our place in the column was worse than being too close. At crossroads and "Y" intersections, our Jay Hawk MPs were stationed to point to the right direction. As dark came on, they waved shielded lamps.

Sometime during the night, we left Germany and crossed back into Belgium. Hour after hour the column rolled on, sometimes at speed, then at stop-and-go. That's when we had to stay awake, in fear that the column would start without us!

Late that night, we passed through a good-sized town. I asked the MP at a street corner, "Where are we, soldier?" He said we were in Spa. I knew then that we were in Belgium and probably getting close to the action. From what we heard, there was no definite front line. Instead there was troop movement in all directions. Many of the US units were going in the opposite direction to ours. Some outfits were obviously trying to get away from the enemy, but our mission was to find and destroy him.

The weather was awful. Low clouds were dripping rain and fog. Then the fog became a Scotch mist, which means the drops of water were a little larger than usual. Ice started to form on the steel of our vehicle and in spots on the road.

South of Spa, the tanks and half-tracks of Task Force Lovelady to which we were assigned passed through a deep forest. On both sides of the road there were stacks of Jerry gas cans. It was a big gas dump. In the dim light, several groups of service GIs silently watched us as we rolled by. They were black troops, doing a great job trying to get the thousands of Jerry cans of gas loaded onto trucks and out of the Germans' grasp. Their eyes followed us. None of them waved and we didn't wave either, but we felt they were saying, "We hope you save all our asses, buddy."

Beyond the gas dump, the area was very quiet. Nothing moved except us. At some crossroads and at a bend in the road, anti-aircraft guns had been manned and set up in defensive positions pointing down the road in the direction in which we were going.

These guns were not looking for aircraft. They were waiting for German tanks.

Thin light filtered through the trees at daybreak and we could see that we were in lousy tank country. The roads were narrow and twisted between steep hills covered with trees. Our vehicles were forced to stay in a column where the only maneuver available was going forward or backwards.

E Co. 33rd Armor tanks were leading the Task Force with us right behind, when the tanks met a German column at a bend in the road. In a few minutes all the enemy vehicles were burning wrecks, and prisoners were being handed back toward the rear.

At full daylight, we ran into another, larger group and again left them burning and exploding. This appeared to be a major supply column, and was made up of many trucks, vans, and horse-drawn carts. It's amazing how many horses the German army used. It was a terrible sight to see them being slaughtered in their traces when our tank shells smashed into the convoy.

Out on the plains of France, when this happened, the French came running out with knives and pots.

The column eased past the last demolished enemy vehicles and rolled South, still seeking the enemy. Our mission, we had guessed, was to find the advancing enemy and to stop him. My track was just behind the lead group of the 33rd tanks. It was a four-tank platoon, and I was surprised that we Dogfaces were not called to ride their back decks. Not that we were eager to climb on those moving targets.

Our tanks rolled into the edge of a small town when full daylight filled the valleys. I say full daylight, but that was only by the clock. Fog and mist still covered the hills and valleys and cut visibility to nearly nothing.

To our left was a high railroad embankment and to the right of the road, a row of houses. Then to the left front we saw a tunnel under the tracks and up ahead a blown bridge. Our tanks stopped, and I suppose they were talking over their next move by radio. We sat in our half-track and watched the hills around us and the silent houses, ready for any sign of the enemy.

Just as the tanks rumbled into motion, we were ordered to dismount. I thought that we would be climbing onto a tank, but the lead Sherman turned into the railroad viaduct and the rest followed. Sgt. Savinski came up and told me to follow them into the tunnel. Vories drove off with E-12 to hide her beside a building. I spread the men on both sides of the road, and then started to advance into the viaduct.

Once inside, we saw that there were two railroad tracks passing over the road. A roadside pole had a board with an arrow pointed toward Stavelot.

It was a nervous squad that walked on that road. I had sent Stevans and Cordell ahead as scouts, and they waved us forward. The feeling we all held was that we were walking into an ambush, and it was a brighter world when we reached the other side.

A small building appeared on the right. We passed it cautiously as we saw our tanks go around a bend up ahead. About fifty feet past the house, small arms fire started to snap all around us. I waved the men into the ditch on the left as we tried to see where the fire was coming from. It appeared to be from a point near a small bridge to our right front. It was then we saw a river was flowing to the right of our position; that was the reason for the blown bridge. I told the squad to hold their fire; we couldn't spot any target at that moment.

Heavy firing started up ahead of us where the tanks were. They were out of sight, but there was plenty of noise coming from that direction and from across the river. Then our Lt. Davenport came walking down the middle of the road. He passed us, and then I shouted to the men, "OK, let's go. We can't let him go up there by himself."

We climbed out of the ditch and went down the road with Davenport. After we'd gone about one hundred yards, the small arms fire started again—the snapping bullets were very close. Again, we all headed for the ditch, including the lieutenant.

Across from my position, just before I hit the ditch, I had seen an American gun crew clustered around their 57mm anti-tank gun. They were all dead. It looked like they had been machine-gunned, because I couldn't see any big wounds. Also, their bodies hadn't been looted. The pockets of the jackets and pants weren't turned inside out as was normal when the Krauts found a dead American. These guys were just lying there behind the gun shield.

I learned later they were from the 526th Armored Infantry and had been helpful in slowing the German column of Kampfgruppe Peiper. Their names were

Donald Hollenbeck, Dallas Buchanan, James Higgins and Lillard McCollum.

Our Lt. had a walkie-talkie, and after talking into it, he motioned to us to start back to the viaduct. When the small arms fire eased a bit, I sent the men back by twos. We assembled on the other side of the railroad tracks, and then got orders to climb the embankment on the reverse slope and dig in along the track line. That we did, but the digging wasn't easy. There were layers of gravel before we got down to earth. Big shovels from E-12 and the tanks helped us get the line dug in.

When the squad holes were deep enough, I went down to the street to see if we had a basement to live in. I was told to take one across from the viaduct opening, and I found Charley Vories and Eleanor already parked in an alley near the house.

"How deep is the basement?" I asked Charley.

He said, "It's OK, but you won't like what you see in there, Sarge."

I went into the building, which was a couple of stories high, and walked down the entrance hall. On the right was a room with an X-ray machine. At least I think it was one; it could have been a fluoroscope machine. Then I noticed blood flowing from the kitchen. On the floor was an elderly woman, a bullet hole in her head. Charley said, "Next door there is an old man and young boy, same thing with them—a bullet in the head. I heard there are more all over the town. The SS went through here yesterday."

We covered the woman and then had to find newspaper to put on the blood in the hall. We were slipping in it as we walked through the area. In years to come I would finally learn the identity of the old woman, shot by the SS. It was Madame Georgine Corbisier, a 55-year-old woman. I also learned the names of the nineteen other civilians whose bodies were scattered all over town.

I was examining the rest of the house when I ran into a civilian, a Belgian. I didn't ask where he came from, but I did ask him, "What is this town?"

He understood and took me over to a wall map. "Ici Trois-Ponts" he said. Then he disappeared.

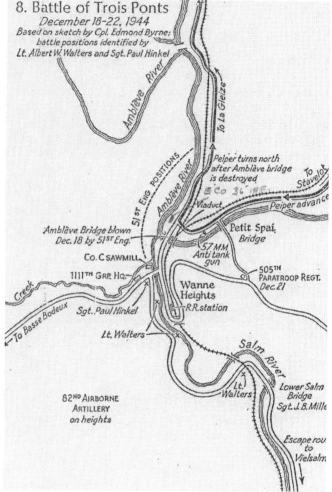

8. Battle of Trois Ponts
December 18-22, 1944
Based on sketch by Cpl. Edmond Byrne;
battle positions identified by
Lt. Albert W. Walters and Sgt. Paul Hinkel

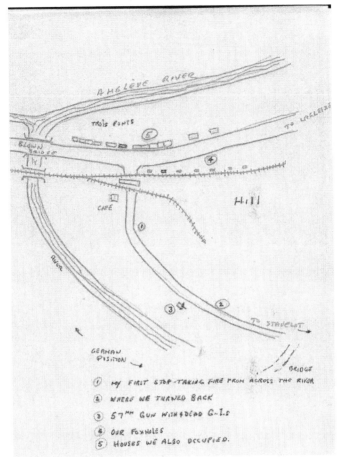

(Sketch by James K. Cullen showing some landmarks of the action in Trois Ponts, where E company was trapped from December 20, to December 24, 1944. They were eventually relieved by the 30th Infantry Division.)

(Photo of Trois Ponts.)

I brought some of the men down in rotation to settle into the basement, and then at dusk, we all stood guard on the hill in case the Krauts tried to attack. Our light tanks had placed themselves so that they had a clear field of fire at the viaduct opening. Then I set a guard schedule and waited.

Down on the street, I went over to the Lt. and asked him "When are our tanks coming back, sir?" He said, "They're not. When they went around the bend, the last tank was hit from across the river, then the lead tank, and then the two in the middle. Lt. Hope, the platoon leader, was killed. I don't know how many survived."

"Was it a Kraut tank that hit them?"

He replied that he didn't know, but it could have been a couple of anti-tank guns, or one tank with a fast loader. "Anyway, anything that comes through the viaduct will be enemy. This roadblock is important in stopping the Jerrys so stay on the alert up by the railroad tracks; they could send infantry."

My reply was, "Yes, Sir."

The weather was colder by morning and the fog

persisted. The squad stood guard up by the tracks, came down the hill in pairs, ate, slept, and wrote letters— the usual things. Our sector was sort of peaceful, but off to our right across the river, there was a good fight going on. We knew the 82nd Airborne was on the big hill behind and to the right of us, and we figured they were involved in all the noise. We could hear the two different cyclic rates in the machine-gun fire. The rapid, burp gun style of the German fire predominated. The American machine gun sounds were fewer and slower.

Then our own trouble started. Mortar shells started to come in on us. The shells hit all over the little town and in the field toward the river. The houses, thank goodness, had several stories and although the upper floors took a beating, the basements were good protection for us. Of course, we weren't in them; with the mortars, we expected a ground attack, so we had to maintain the defensive line at the tracks.

Jerry would throw a bunch of shells, and then do nothing for hours. During this time, we stayed in the holes and waited.

I had a copy of one of our Army issue books, a small volume that fit nicely into the pocket of our jackets. It was C. S. Forester's "The Gun." I read it when I wasn't watching the hills above us. It was a great book. Combat wasn't always blood and thunder—there were quiet periods in between the panic, the horror, and the terror.

I came down from the defense line that night and went across the road to a garage-type building. Some GIs had built a fire in a fifty-five-gallon drum and were clustered around it. I went in to get warm too. As I approached the fire, I saw one of the soldiers looking at me. I recognized him.

"Bob?"

He answered, "Jim?"

It was Bob Severance from Brooklyn, NY. We had attended public school PS 185 together. Small world. We chatted briefly. He was with an Engineer outfit. Then he was called; they were moving out.

The Krauts knew they couldn't force the roadblock. If one tank started through the tunnel, it would be hit and stopped. That would put the stopper in the bottle; the road would be jammed tight. Instead, they brought troops over the little bridge we had seen in the distance and started overland. They had to climb the steep hills in front of us, but once they got up there, they were looking down our throats. We had to get out of the foxholes and work from the houses.

From the upper floors we could see the German infantry as they crept through the woods. They didn't make great targets, but we could shoot at them, and we did. Our fire, and the fact that they couldn't come over the railroad tracks without being perfect targets, persuaded them to slip sideways towards our left front. There were fewer houses at the end of the village and thicker woods. In doing so, they captured the road we had come in on. We were cut off from the rest of T.F. Lovelady and were trapped.

The Krauts were in front of us; behind us was the cold Amblève River, but there wasn't any panic on our part. We did have a good strong house to stay in, and it made an excellent observation and firing post. We had K and C rations, and there were a few extra K ration cases on the tanks. Thanks to the Belgian women, we had canned, preserved fruit and vegetables that we found in the basement, so we weren't that worried. We could hold out and keep our roadblock in place. That was our assignment.

In 1998, I read that there was talk about our surrender because we were surrounded and low on ammunition. I disputed that, even though the quote had come from Lt. Col. Lovelady. His H.Q. wasn't in Trois-Ponts, and I don't think he was aware of our true situation. We had no thoughts of surrender.

The mortars started again. Houses were hit time after

time, but there was no fire. Usually concentrated fire like that would start one or two roof tops burning. The shells did damage, though. During a quiet period, the officers were standing in the street: Maj. Stallings, Lt. McCord (our CO), Lt. Alejandro (3rd Platoon), Lt. McGee (2nd Platoon), and Lt. Davenport (1st Platoon). They were talking about the possibility of us going to help the 82nd.

Without warning, a mortar shell dropped right beside them and Lt. McCord was hit and died immediately. We dragged his body into the hall of our house and covered him. None of the others was hurt. Later that day, his body disappeared from the hallway, and when I asked what happened, someone said that the medics took him.

I guess Stallings decided to ask the 82nd for some suppressing mortar fire on the German positions on the hills in front of us. They started to lob shells over our heads into the enemy lines. The first barrage landed on target. The next salvo had a single short round which dropped into one of the 2nd Platoon's half-tracks and blew it to hell.

The days passed. We had come into the town on the 20th and knew that Christmas was around the corner but didn't really think much about it. Our concentration was here in the house we were in, and the crossroad we were defending. If Christmas came, we couldn't do much about it anyway. Hell, we had had our Christmas up in Germany.

We read, ate K rations, watched the woods in front of us, and fired at Jerry when he appeared in the trees. At night we posted guards all around in case the Krauts tried to hit us from the river side. Our light tanks tried to break out of the trap but were beaten back. Then we heard the 30th Division was going into an attack to break the German roadblock, so we waited and watched. The weather had remained the same for days—fog, mist, rain, low clouds and cold. It got colder, and the temperature dropped below 30.

Toward the middle of one afternoon, the happy word

came down; the 30th had broken through the German lines! We could be re-supplied with food and ammunition, and maybe some reinforcements. Our casualties hadn't been that high, but it was always good to have company. The Krauts were still attacking all along the line even though we had stopped them at this point.

But we didn't need the reinforcements; our orders were to pull out and go back North. Our task force had been attached to the 30th Division and then the XVIII Airborne Corps, and now it was attached to the 21st Army group, run by the British Gen. Montgomery. "Monty" wanted to straighten the line, and we were salient, a military term that means sticking out like a sore thumb. We weren't upset about getting out of there, so we quickly started packing the vehicles. The Krauts were still shelling us, and we kept our ears open for the first mortar shell. Climbing aboard Eleanor, we were set to get out on the road.

Vories started the engine, slipped it into gear, and nothing happened. From the ring mount I looked down and asked "What's the matter? Can't you get it into gear?"

"No, Sarge, she's in gear, but she won't move."

All up and down the street we heard tank and half-track engines roaring, but none of them moved. We were all frozen solid to the ground. With all the rain and fog, the ground was very wet, then for the last two days the temperature had dropped below freezing. We were stuck.

Out came crow bars, shovels, and picks. By chipping at the ice with the tools, combined with rocking the half-track forward and back, we finally broke loose. The column formed up and we started out of Trois Ponts. I think that all our casualties, including Lt. McCord, were brought out with the Task Force, but I'm not positive.

By then it was dark and still foggy. Shells started to drop in on the road as if the Jerrys were saying goodbye. I was trying to keep Eightball's cat's eye lights in sight when shells came crashing in on the road. By this time Vories was speeding up to avoid the incoming and keep up with

Eightball, who was also moving faster. We hit a shell hole with the front wheel and bounced. I went up into the air, and then fell back, but before I hit, I tucked my chin into my chest. I knew the sharp steel ring mount for the .50 caliber machine gun was right in front of me. My helmet took the blow, but I was stunned. I dropped to the bottom of the cockpit and lay there. Gonzalez yelled "Cullen's dead!" and climbed on top of me to see ahead. I wasn't unconscious, just semi-out, and then quickly recovered. I shouted, "Get off my ass damn you."

He got off.

CHAPTER FOURTEEN
What the Hell Is That?

In the dark and fog it was hard to see E-11's lights, so we crept up closer on the icy road. Vories and I were keeping him in sight and following him pretty well when E-11 started to slide sideways. We went right with him, into a big ditch. The rest of the column passed us in the night.

Our crew, and E 11's crew, crossed the road to a small farmhouse, and were welcomed by the Belgian family who lived there. We sat in the warm room drinking a little wine and terrible coffee for a few hours. Someone said, "Hey, this is Christmas Eve."

Actually, it was nearly midnight and close to Christmas Day and as we realized this, we sort of shrugged to each other. It was just another day. An Army 6 x 6 truck with a cable pulled us both out of the ditch.

With our vehicles back on the road, we drove on through that Christmas Eve night, guided at crossroads by MPs who knew where we were supposed to go—we sure didn't. Dawn was in the sky when our two lost half-tracks pulled into the Regimental assembly area. We were waved towards a spot near some trees where the rest of E Co. was coiled. The squad got out onto the ground and into sleeping bags. I asserted my rank and claimed a choice spot on Eleanor's hood. The weather was very cold, and her hood was nice and warm.

After a few hours of sleep, we were roused by the noise of engines and a bright light. We couldn't believe our eyes—it was the sun at last. We hadn't seen it for days. The sky was clear and blue but soon became hazy with the contrails of the planes flying over. The big trails were bombers, and the small neat ones that curved and circled were the fighters. The bombers were all heading east, so we knew they had to be ours. Seeing all the air activity, I wondered whether we shouldn't dig a few slit trenches in case we were bombed, but the men talked me out of it; anyway, the ground was getting too hard to get a hole started. We figured that out when we did our latrine duty. To go to the bathroom we had to do some chopping on the ground to make our own little "shit hole."

Since it *was* Christmas, we thought we might get a hot meal and chatted about what it might be. Half of us thought it might be turkey, and the rest voted for ham. The question was settled when a 6 x 6 truck came by and threw down boxes of K and C rations. Along with the boxes was the order to get ready to move out within two hours.

Merry Christmas!

We loaded the rations and waited. Later, orders came to roll, so we followed the leader out of the field and onto the single road. This time the direction was west.

I was in the ring mount looking up at the airplanes with a pair of liberated Jerry binoculars. I blinked when something zipped across the lens. It was an airplane, but the fastest one I'd ever seen. I had to move my head quickly to try to keep up with it. I said out loud, "What the hell is that?" I was thinking to myself *Was that really an aircraft? It disappeared so fast.* Little did I know that I had seen my first jet—a German one at that.

The winter days are short in Belgium, and light was

fading when we rolled into our position. The 75th Infantry Division had just arrived in Europe and had been rushed into the line. Our assignment was to back them up and to support their flanks. A small farmhouse sat beside the road we were given to defend, so I had Vories pull Eleanor up close to the house, and we put the heavy canvas winter cover on her.

To the right of the road there was a field about thirty yards wide, bordered by a row of brush and hedge. I told the men to dig two-man holes when I placed them along the hedge. Two-man holes are warmer. My hole, with Collier, was near the house and the last hole was down by a bend in the road. We had a good field of fire if anything approached our position, but all we had to fire was our BAR and our rifles. We did not have any Bazookas; they were not issued to us.

The weather got worse. The temperature kept dropping lower each day. With no thermometers, we could only judge the temperature by how fast water froze, and it was pretty quick.

At night, each hole was on guard and alert on a schedule I would set. The two men would stand their time, then wake the next two.

Our sleeping bags were OK when we slept spoon fashion with any extra blankets over the top of us. Of course, we had on our complete uniform including boots. We were in a front-line position and had to be ready at a moment's notice. Just getting out of the bags though, if we were attacked, would be difficult and time consuming. The bags zipped up to the neck and had no quick release zippers. To get out of the bag in a hurry, we had to kick the bag down as we tried to pull ourselves loose. Many times, we would sleep on top of the bag with blankets over us. It was safer that way, but colder.

We were in that position for two days when we heard a lot of small arms activity taking place over the hill to our left. That's where the 75th Division was, and they were catching hell. The firing, which sounded like a lot of fast Kraut fire, kept up most of the night and part of the next day.

That night, Christmas sort of caught up with us. Hot food in Mermite cans was brought to us. It was unloaded into the house, and those off guard clustered around. The cans were opened, and Reuben Kline, our Jewish guy, looked in and said, "Wow, it's chicken."

It was ham, but we agreed with him anyway. Dinner was great!

Later when I was asleep in our foxhole, the ground underneath me heaved and there was a tremendous explosion near us.

"What the hell was that?" Collier and I scrambled out of the sleeping bags and blankets and jumped up on the ground. There was a cloud of smoke out on the road, but everything was still except for the patter of debris falling all around us. There had been some random shells falling during our time in this position, but this was no ordinary shell. I went down the line to check the men. The night wasn't too dark, and I could make out things, but dimly. Vernon Spores was standing in his hole; he had been on alert and I asked him what he had seen.

"Five GIs came down the road, Sergeant, carrying racks of mines. When they were near the bend, they blew up. There was a flash and they just disappeared. I had my head out of the hole, on guard, and I ducked. When I looked up, they were gone."

There was nothing we could do, so we all went back into the foxholes and slept until first light. At the scene of the explosion, in the middle of the road, there was a dark splash where the asphalt had been battered. At the edge of the field, a wire fence held shreds of uniforms and skin. I went back to the house and one of the men said, "Look on top of the track." We had the winter cover on E-12, and I got up onto the hood. She was covered with small pieces of flesh, each about the size of a quarter. I cleaned the canvas of all the bits and pieces of the five men.

Later in the day I went up into the brush with my shovel to relieve myself. I found half a pelvic bone and not too far away a torso with a sweater still on it. When we left the field, we passed the word that there were parts of bodies on the hill. I hoped it would get to Grave Registration, but even if it did, there would still be five GI's missing in action.

Half of the squad, including me, was out in the foxhole line when we heard a growing rumble from the sky overhead. It was a fairly clear day, and we saw flights of bombers going over—headed east towards Germany. They were B-24s. I didn't know it at the time but my brother, Martin, was training to fly these big airplanes and would take one to the Pacific war.

The planes, with their distinctive barn-door tails, roared across the sky. We could feel the vibration of their noise on our skin. Wave after wave went by as German flak started to blossom in black cloud puffs amongst the planes. The airplanes stayed in a straight flight path.

Then one was hit. It slowly came out of the formation in a wide spiral. One parachute appeared, then another dot left the plane and it became another chute, the B-24's spiral became tighter and tighter, and we could trace it now with the smoke trail it was leaving.

We blinked our eyes when the airplane disappeared in a blinding, bright, flash. Out of the white cloud that hung there in the sky, pieces of debris fell past the two parachutes. Through the roar of the rest of the bombers, we felt the thud of the explosion when it reached us from fifteen thousand feet up where the squadron stayed on its course.

I looked at the smoke in the sky, and then at the large smear on the road in front of us where our five engineers disappeared. The B-24 carried a crew of ten, and only two escaped. That was thirteen to add to the day's casualty list in the Ardennes.

That night we got snow for the first time. We had heard that some areas in the Ardennes already had snow, but all we had was bitter cold. Now we had both. Thankfully, the next day we were relieved. We climbed into Eleanor after we brushed her off and we took off for a new assembly area. The Division was out of the action, but we knew the respite wouldn't last long. The Krauts were still moving west even though they had been stopped on the northern shoulder where we were.

CHAPTER FIFTEEN
Happy New Year

New Year's Day passed cold and clear. The division was preparing for action, but as usual, we were the last to know what was going on. The snow fell several more times. We now had about a foot with a thin layer of ice from an ice storm. The Battalion moved again, and this time we were told that a big attack was in the works. The 2nd Armored and our Division, with the 84th and 83rd Infantry Divisions attached, would be heading south to cut into the flank of the German forces. The two armored divisions would run on parallel tracks and hopefully, we would cut the Krauts off close to the line where they started their counter-attack on December 16th.

Combat Command B moved us to another assembly area, and we became part of Task Force McGeorge. Colonel Lovelady was ill with influenza that had hit many of the troops. We also started to get warnings about trench foot, which none of my men got, even though the latest shoepacs never reached us. The uniform of the day was the regular olive drab wool shirt and pants with the addition of wool long Johns, and a wool sweater, gloves, and underwear. Winter gear was twelve buckle galoshes and had been Engineer's Mackinaws. These were good coats that gave us mobility and warmth. They had a blanket lining, and a shawl collar, but some ass in the Quarter Master Corps decided we had to have overcoats to keep out the cold weather. They took away our Mackinaws and issued the longer overcoats that were made of heavy wool and reached down to our knees. If we were standing still, in formation, the coats would be great, but we were not standing still. We had to climb onto the Sherman Tanks and get in and out of our half-tracks. The coats made that hard to do. Even worse was the two feet of ice we accumulated on the bottom of the coats. The icy skirt came from the deep snow that had started to fill the field and roads. Some GIs took their bayonets and hacked off a foot of the bottom of their coats.

But we had bigger worries than our clothing. The final attack was on, and January 3 was the day that we headed south. Instead of mounting a tank, we crossed the line of departure and started out on foot through the deep snow.

The attack started late in the day for some reason. The squad was spread out, in case of shells, as we went forward. We weren't at the point, so we just followed the squads ahead of us. The sun dropped out of sight as we entered a dark, thick forest. Up at the point of attack (it was D Co.), trouble started with a roadblock protected by mortars. We were told to defend where we were. That meant we tried to find depressions in the snowy ground where we could form a semi-circle and settle for the night.

We tried to scrape deeper holes, but the ground was too hard. Guard was set, and we tried to sleep, but the cold made it difficult. The wind came in gusts, shaking the trees, and sending big chunks of snow down on us. It was bad, but the falling snow was better than mortar shells. When we wanted to smoke a cigarette, we pulled a blanket over our head then lit the smoke. The blanket was to hide the flare of the match from the Krauts. We got the blanket from a pile of rations, sleeping bags, and blankets that had been brought forward to us.

In the dark and cold, most of us didn't try to eat. Maybe nibble on crackers from a K ration. The rest of the meal was frozen, and the only way to thaw the meat can was to put it in your armpit—not likely! So, we fitfully slept and shivered and waited for daylight.

At first light, we were moving again, but stiffly from the long, cold night spent lying in the snow. Our overcoats with their bottom coating of ice clattered as we walked. Before we started moving, we ate some K rations; we heated coffee in our canteen cup by punching two holes in the bottom of the wax carton from the K ration and set the top on fire. Water for the instant coffee was snow that we melted because our canteen water was frozen. The blessed heat got our blood moving, but we had to watch our fingers; they were numb and couldn't feel when we touched the hot canteen cup. We didn't need blisters to add to our misery.

The platoon waded through the foot-deep snow in extended formation. We heard that D Co. had taken a small village to our left, and we were to bypass that place and attack a larger one farther south. The march was stop-and-go as the scouts up forward did their job. The trees hampered their efforts, but we did make progress in the right direction. We learned that our target was Regné, a large village in the low hills ahead.

Late in the day, we came out of some tree cover into a large field, heard a rumble to our right, and saw some Shermans coming at an angle towards us. We didn't pay attention to them until they suddenly opened fire at our column with their machine guns. The tracers in the dim light were bright and frightening as they headed towards us. With bullets cracking all around us, we hit the snow. When the gunners shifted their fire, some of us jumped up, waving and yelling to stop them, and all that got us was another shower of tracers. Down we went again. This time, the GI ahead of me had the heel taken off his boot by a bullet. Then, suddenly they stopped. We shouted and swore at them and wished they would go fight their war someplace else.

Regné was just ahead when we "dug in" for the night. A few shells came in to harass us, but we caught some sleep. When you're cold and exhausted, you can sleep anyplace, any time.

Early the next morning E Co. went on the attack with our platoon in the lead, and my squad on point. I looked at the little town with the houses scattered along a road that ran across from left to right from the edge of the woods. It looked peaceful and quiet. Nothing moved, so we started across the sloping field toward the houses. I sent Cordell and Stevens out as point, and we followed when they reached a wire fence at the edge of town. I waved them on into the village.

As we moved among the buildings, the rest of the platoon came down, and we occupied the town of Regné. We were told to grab a basement, and we took a house at the south end which had a nice, deep basement. Outside the house, a foxhole was dug to use at night for guard, then we settled in for the next order.

(Regne, Belgium. E Company took the town during the January counter-attack.)

Before long, shells started to explode in the village, so we knew that the Germans were aware of our position. It wasn't heavy or frequent, just one or two at a time, then a long pause, then several blasts. The shells were heavy caliber, and we could hear them coming in plenty of time. Except for the outpost near the house, we stayed in the basement and did the usual—sleep, eat, smoke, and wait.

I was called to the Command Post for something. It was about five hundred yards away across an open village square, in a large farmhouse. On the way I passed a GI from another squad standing guard at a corner of a house. We nodded and exchanged a few words. Finished with whatever I was called for, I waited at the CP for fifteen or twenty minutes while a few big shells crashed into the area. Then I started back to our house and saw the GI I had seen before, but he was lying in the snow. I checked him out; he was dead. There was a black smudge in the snow nearby where the shell that killed him had hit. I guess he didn't hear it in time.

Late in the day, company trucks brought mail to us for the first time since Germany. We got letters and packages that had been sent to arrive in time for Christmas. When we opened the boxes, what a sight it was—cakes of all kinds, dried fruit, chocolate bars, cigarettes and sweets. Our families didn't miss a thing. After we read our letters, we hit the holiday packages hard. Some were battered and torn from their journey—probably three months coming through the Army Postal System, but that didn't stop us. We ate, and ate, and looked for more. We ate stale cookies and biscuits, and those made by a loving girlfriend that tasted awful. It was a late Christmas party, but we made a great time of it in our deep basement. Our Christmas music was an occasional German shell landing outside.

The squad paid for it though. That night, everyone was hit with heartburn first, then diarrhea. Some guys threw up. I was out in the guard outpost when I got mine—the burning sensation in my throat followed by a mad scramble trying to get out of my gear; belt, ammo bandolier and harness, dig through my overcoat to my pants, to my Long Johns before I could get to the business of the moment. Then two Jerry shells came whistling in and banged about two hundred yards away. The hell with the shells; I was trying to dig my toilet paper out of my helmet and get my ass out of the cold. That was a memorable night in Regné.

After the spasms and cramps died away everyone recovered, so we knew we hadn't been poisoned. We figured we just ate too many goodies after so many weeks of solid nutritious army K rations, and not too many of those either.

From Regné, we went south along a rather narrow road. My 2nd squad was on point as we marched on one side of the road. It was a cold, clear day with fresh snow. Every once in a while, a few shells came in near the road, but most of them went rushing overhead back towards Regné. I told the men to be ready to go to the ditch if the shells got close, but we didn't want to walk in it. The Krauts liked to sow the ditches with anti-personnel mines.

Several farmhouses along the road were cleared by us very carefully, because the farmers were hiding in their basements. We passed one house, with another in the distance, when our scouts signaled trouble ahead. Crouching low, I ran up to the scouts with the squad coming up behind me.

On the other side of the road to our left front, there were two Krauts standing in the ditch by a stone wall looking out into the field. They didn't see us, but their machine pistols were up at the ready.

I said, "Pick one."

Three or four of us took aim and fired. They both went down. We waited a second, and then Wes Pitzer, who spoke some German, shouted "Raus! Raus!" and to our surprise, one Kraut stood up. He had his arms up and was staring down at his buddy. Apparently, we had all aimed at the same soldier.

We sent the single Jerry back toward Regné. Then we saw what the two Krauts were looking at. Out in the field was a body that looked like a GI. An arm dressed in olive drab came up and tried to wave and we were certain it was an American. Off to the right was an American light tank which appeared abandoned. The GI in the field waved again and I looked at Roy Plummer. He knew what we had to do.

Slinging our M1s over our backs, we ran across the road, over a wire fence, and out into the deep snow on the field. Any minute we expected to be hit.

The GI was about one hundred feet beyond the road and lying on his stomach. When we got to him he was gasping and a little blue. When we saw the blood on his back, and the sucking wound when we opened his jacket, we knew we had to hurry. Roy and I got our arms under him and dragged him back to the road, expecting our own bullet in the back any second. It is a terrible, nerve-shattering feeling to think that a Kraut might have his sight on your head or your back and his finger squeezing the trigger. It's probably better for the nerves to hear a shot go past your head rather than wait for the shot that never comes.

We made it without incident then sent word back for the medic. When he came up, we continued our combat patrol. Later we learned that F Co., from our 2nd Battalion had attacked the area with the light tanks from the 33rd Armor, and he must have been an F Co. GI. What happened to him or the tank, we didn't know.

After we left that field and walked down the road, I asked Roy if he was as afraid of being hit while we were in the middle of the field as I was. He replied that every muscle in his body was tense, just waiting for the bullet! We laughed—and agreed that it was a hairy moment.

The weather turned bad in the afternoon; clouds first, then more snow and wind. Then the Company was ordered off the road and up into the hills. We were to take and hold the high ground while the tanks maintained their attack along the road. The deep snow was lousy for walking; we were exhausted when we arrived at the top of a tree-filled hill. The snow in the trees, as usual, gave us problems. One was the frequent neck full of snow we got as we went between the big pines. The snow seemed to cling to the tree branch until someone was directly under it, and then a big lump of wet snow would fall, hit the helmet, and pour down the neck, resulting in a lot of swearing. The second thing was the way the snow-laden trees muffled sound. We were always alert for the sound of a mortar or incoming shells—or the enemy himself—but in deep woods, little was heard.

The snow continued to fall, swirling around us and the trees in the strong wind. When we were moving up into the hills, the cold wasn't too bad, but when we stopped because of trouble ahead, we suffered. One of my men, Earl Cordell, was from the south, and he seemed to feel it worse than the rest of us.

He also had a unique problem. He told us that, "A couple of years ago, I had a bad case of hemorrhoids and they operated on my ass. When they did that, they cut my 'puckering string.' So now, when I have to shit, I have to go now!"

We couldn't laugh at him because in the snow and cold he had a serious problem.

CHAPTER SIXTEEN
Schoolyard Stand Off

The woods seemed to get deeper as we walked toward our objective, which was on a compass course. Logging trails were cut through the forest, but we crossed them at right angles, so they were no help to our march. My squad was in the lead in the column when we crossed one of these trails and went on for about fifty yards. I was in the middle of the squad when the word was passed up to me. "Sergeant, something seems to have happened to our rear." Stopping the men, I went back along our path and came to my last man, Gonzales. He said he thought he'd heard firing behind us, and he couldn't find the men from the 3rd squad. I told him to come with me and we went back toward the logging trail. Just as I was stepping out onto the trail, a German came from the left. My rifle was at my hip when I saw him. He had a rifle slung on his shoulder, but I didn't wait. I fired, and he went down. When he scrambled around to get at his weapon, I shot again. Gonzales and I stood still looking and waiting for more Krauts to come along, but none did.

In that moment of stillness, I realized how frightened I was. My mouth was like dry sandpaper, so I grabbed some snow from a branch, while I kept my eyes on the trail, and stuffed it into my mouth.

Then across the trail, a GI from the 3rd squad appeared. I said, "What the hell happened to you people?"

"We were just crossing the trail when a Kraut platoon came along. They shot the hell out of us and we ran back into the woods."

"Was anyone hurt?"

"No, at least I don't think so. I don't know."

I sent Gonzales back to get the rest of our squad, and we all gathered by the trail. We talked over the possibility of more Jerrys coming at us from the side, so we decided to go down the trail to see where they were coming from. In column, the squads went about one hundred yards when we came to a clearing. As we emerged from the woods—a platoon of Germans came out of the opposite woods, about a hundred feet away!

They stopped when they saw us. We slowly spread our ranks and faced them with our rifles raised and I shouted, "Drop your weapons." And some of my men joined me, shouting to the enemy to "give up, komme raus", and other things. As we yelled at them, the Germans were shouting at us. I suppose it was the same things we were shouting. I thought we were making progress, because some of them looked as if they would be happy to drop their rifles. Others were looking more menacing and seemed to be about to shoot.

This yelling and shouting, like kids in a school yard, went on for about three minutes when some movement caught my eye—off to our right, at the edge of the big clearing. I saw three Sherman tanks come out of the woods. They didn't slow down, but just kept rolling and then started firing their machine guns—at us, not at the Germans. That quickly broke up the party. Their bullets were splintering branches and trees around us as we ran for protection. I went for a depression in the ground behind a tree, but someone was faster, and I landed on top of him. We had no radio to talk to the tanks and all we could do was wave our arms to "cease fire." They finally did, after we had one GI dead and two wounded. The dead man, not from my squad, was hit in the groin and bled to death.

The Jerrys and the tanks all disappeared, and we left, too, after we made sure the medics were working on the wounded. As we got back onto the trail, we talked about the unfairness of being hit by our own troops.

Unfortunately, these things happened.

Still up on the high ground, we assembled in bivouac near Ottré, and for a day or two we were out of contact with the enemy. Our half-tracks came up to us, with our sleeping bags and extra blankets. The area was relatively quiet. The Regiment's kitchens actually brought up hot food. Only an occasional shell came into our area, and by that time we were well trained in hearing and locating where an in-coming was and where it would land. You could see everyone tense up at the first whisper of a shell, then it was either "run for cover" or "relax."

The sound of a jeep starting was bad for all of our nerves, collectively. It had the same whispery note of a shell on its way in, but one that we couldn't locate for a few seconds.

Mail came up, we wrote letters, and aside from the cold and snow it was a good couple of days. We learned the 83rd Infantry Division was scheduled to pass through our lines and take over the attack.

I don't know which regiment of the 83rd Division went through our area, but they passed close to us. We were "armored infantry" and they were "infantry." They were "foot sloggers" and we were "blitz doughs." Both of us went under many other names, but basically, we did the same job. We were the troops who were out in front of the rest of the Army. We were the "sharp end of the spear."

I stood by our half-track and watched one 83rd Division Platoon as they sat in the snow waiting for orders to move on. They were a pretty sorry lot. They had the same heavy overcoats we had, with a fringe of ice on the bottom. I saw one GI was wearing a sleeping bag. He had cut holes for arms, cut off the bottom, and was wearing the whole thing over his overcoat.

Every GI in that unit had some beard; the older guys (aged 25-26) had thick, black beards. The younger ones (19-20) were just shadow beards, but all of them had dirty, dark faces with runny noses and weary eyes. They looked tired and worn out.

Then I looked at my own men, and I realized that there was no difference in the two groups of soldiers. We were the "P.B.I." as the British called us; the "Poor Bloody Infantry." We were dirty, smelly, and looked like hell, but we were fighting a cold, dirty war. Later some German prisoners were marched by and they looked no different, aside from the color of their uniforms.

Our next objective after this "Rest and Recreation" was a small nameless village that we took without trouble, because there were no Germans.

We kept going, struggling through the snowy woods, and went into a night attack on another, larger, nameless village. This time Jerry was waiting for us. Some of our Sherman tanks joined us as we came out of the woods on our approach. Our tanks started to fire down the road at a German tank, and that tank returned fire in our direction. Small arms and heavy stuff came streaking down the road, and tracers were bouncing in all directions.

CHAPTER SEVENTEEN
Ankle Deep

Buildings started to burn, and we worked our way into the town. Smoke was blowing all around us as we entered the houses. Our squads became mixed in the confusion. Some officers grabbed two of my men and sent them off to check a house, and as I started after them, I saw a large figure appear in a doorway which was filled with smoke. One of the 1st squad GIs ran towards him, thinking it was another GI. Unfortunately, it was a Kraut who promptly fired his burp gun at the GI, shooting off one of the GI's fingers. The smoke then covered the German, and he disappeared before we could return his fire.

There was a lot of noise, flames, smoke, yelling, and shouting. We were trying to clear each room in each house, but it was a bad job. The flickering light of the flames just added to the confusion as we entered the dark houses. Luckily, we didn't meet any more Germans. The ones we saw must have been a rear-guard unit left there to delay us. Suddenly, there were no more shots—even the fires seemed to die down. We realized the Krauts must have pulled out. That was fine with us.

We were told to find a basement for the night; we were going to hold our position. I gathered my men, who were scattered around the village, and we found a deep, dry basement in a small house. I posted one guard outside and we settled in. I had just taken off my leggings, boots, and galoshes and was rubbing my toes before changing socks when Sgt. Cofer came partly down the basement stairs.

"Cullen, get your squad together and come on up out of there." So, I put on my socks and boots and we assembled on the dark road.

I asked Cofer, "What's going on? We were just getting warm!"

"Yeah, I know. Tough shit. One of the officers thinks he heard some Krauts at the other end of town. He wants a patrol to check it out. He thinks he heard something on the right side of the road. Check those houses."

We crossed the road and started down the back ends of the houses. I figured that approach would give us better cover than going down the street side. None of the back doors were locked, and some were broken from the earlier fight. At each house, I would send in a few men while we guarded the outside. Then I went into one and got a shock. As I tried to sneak quietly into the rooms, I heard a clunking noise following me. Every time I moved there was this "clunk."

I realized what it was when I shook my canteen where it hung on my belt. The water in it had frozen solid during the day, and then had partly melted when we were in the warm basement, so the ice was hitting the inside of the canteen every time I took a step.

Back outside, I didn't go into any more of the houses—I was a walking alarm bell! I sent two other men instead.

Then, an unusual disaster struck. There was a small shack behind a house, and I went around it. The deep snow covered the ground as I stepped carefully near the corner. The place smelled terrible, and I figured it must be a pig sty.

Under my left foot, I felt slippery ice. Before I could

shift my weight, the ice broke and my leg went down into liquid; what turned out to be liquid pig shit. It quickly filled my overshoe, and nearly knocked me out with the smell.

We went into two more houses, and then I called a halt. I figured the patrol had done enough, and we headed back to our basement. The squad, though, insisted I wash my boot in the snow and leave it outside before we went back into the basement.

We moved on the next morning; the high ground was still our territory. Third squad was in the lead when we took a small cluster of farm houses. Our people flushed out more than a dozen German soldiers who gave us no resistance. Their helmets were taken off, and then they were lined up in a column and sent back to the rear. As they passed my squad, I saw that one Kraut, with his hands up, had a pair of good-looking gloves. I went over, took the gloves off him, and said, "You won't need these where you're going." They were waterproof shells, shaped like mittens, and fit very well over my GI wool gloves. They were much admired and desired by everyone. My wool gloves stayed dry, and these new gloves even had a trigger finger, although it was too bulky to be able to pull the trigger with my finger inside the glove. All my squad wanted a pair, and they looked at each Kraut, hoping to find a pair of these great new German gloves.

Then, my bubble burst. I learned that the marvelous German gloves of mine were actually GI issue. That lousy Kraut must have taken them off an American prisoner during their initial attack on December 16. At that time, they had captured around seven thousand GIs from the 106th Division alone. With that knowledge, we had some nasty thoughts about our Quartermaster Corps. They also put hundreds of the 99th Division men "in the bag."

CHAPTER EIGHTEEN
Not Again

Late in the day, we were called forward to relieve a platoon that was out at the point. Our whole column had been stopped in our attack by orders from the rear. Perhaps we were too far out in front of the rest of the task force, who were down on the narrow roads. Perhaps we were in danger of being cut off if Jerry came in our flank; it had happened before.

We got up to the position in the deep woods, and I looked around for the squad leader. He came out of the tree line, and we met in the middle of a logging trail. As he came towards me, I looked down the trail. It was on a sloped hill, and down the hill about 150 feet away I could see two soldiers. One was bent over something in the snow. I turned to the squad leader that I was relieving and started asking about the other squad's position and the layout of his foxholes. He gave me a good outline of the area, and where his men were. I continued questioning him, then asked who was in front of us. "No one" he said. "We're out at the point in the forward defensive position."

I asked, "Well, who the hell are those guys?" and pointed down the trail. We both looked down the hill and I saw that the two soldiers were now looking up at us, and that the object on the ground appeared to be a dead GI.

"They're Krauts!" I shouted, and we both ducked back

toward the trees. Instead of our other squad being relieved, they stayed with us and we engaged in a little firefight. We didn't know how many Germans we were fighting—we only saw two, and that is the number they saw of us. Both groups were firing blindly at shadows in the snow.

My squad didn't have time or a chance to dig in; we went prone behind fallen trees. They formed a good line, and I tried to tie into the squad we were relieving. I told the men to fire at anything that moved, and to keep firing. If we had just the two Krauts in front of us, our firing would keep them down. If there were more than two, then we would make them think we were a whole company.

It was getting dark when one of my men was hit. I can't remember his name, just the event. I crawled over to see how he was and saw that I couldn't do anything for him; he wasn't that badly hit. Then I stupidly stood up by a tree to do some observation. I was trying to see where Jerry was by gun flashes but saw nothing.

Then, something hit the tree by my head with a bang and a flash. I was knocked off my feet and down into the snow. My head was ringing like a church bell. I dimly heard Joe Gonzales yell, "Cullen's dead!"

I thought—not again! Maybe one of these times he *will* be right.

I knew I wasn't, but a lot of things went racing through the fog in my mind. Maybe if I stay right here where I am, face down in the snow, everyone will leave and forget me. No more snow, no more freezing fingers and freezing ears, and no more hunger and fear. I'd find a warm basement and dig in there until the war was over.

Savino kept yelling, "Cullen's dead."

I rolled over and said, "Not yet, God damn you!"

I crawled back through the deep snow to the men, then yelled back to the guy that had been wounded. "Get back here, you're not that bad, it's only a scratch."

Actually, he had a pretty good graze on his arm and we called for the medic.

We tried to figure out what they had thrown at me. It could have been a captured GI rifle grenade; it certainly wasn't a Panzerfaust, but whatever it was, my right ear was still ringing, and I had spots of blood on my cheek.

The firing died away, and the other squad went to the rear. We occupied their old foxholes and kept extra alert on guard that night.

It had been a very small action, one of many that were never mentioned in official After-Action Reports.

The next evening, in the long twilight in Europe, we were teamed up with a couple of tank destroyers, probably the 703rd T. D. We were on the edge of a somewhat high ridge, when one of my squad saw a German tank down in the valley. We called the T.D.'s attention to it, and they decided to try a shot at the Jerry.

My squad backed away from the muzzle blast as the T.D. fired. He missed! Then the German tank moved, and we could see his long main tube come up.

The German tank fired, and our T.D. exploded. One guy made it out, wounded and bleeding, and we got him onto a stretcher. I have no idea where the stretcher came from; maybe it was in the T.D. and they used it to sleep on.

Four of us started to run with the wounded man toward a farmhouse. We also wanted to get away from the exploding ammunition in the tank destroyer. As we ran over a small mound, I fell to my knees in the snow, but continued to run on my knees for a good distance. Then I called a halt; we walked the rest of the way.

It might have been the evening of the next day, I can't remember. It was a very cloudy, dark day in any case. We were working our way forward in deep woods—as usual. I had two men out as scouts and could hardly see them in the dim light. When they came to an opening in the woods with a field in front of them, they waved me up to where they were.

"There's something out there in the field, Sarge,"

adding, "It looks strange."

I looked where they pointed and saw a low mass of something covered in snow. Was it a bunker or pillbox?

Then, in the half-light I saw a tail sticking up out of the snow with a swastika on it. It was an airplane, a Jerry bomber. We walked out to it and saw that it was a Heinkel He 111 that had crashed. It had landed flat. I guessed that it had come in with its wheels up; the nose wasn't crushed.

Out on the ground was a flyer's body. He was lying face up and wore a leather flying suit. His face was flat and misshapen as if he had hit something very hard.

We talked about taking his leather suit but saw that every seam in the suit was burst. Maybe he jumped as the plane came down and just happened to be there when his plane hit. But if he did, there was no parachute attached to the body. It was another of the war's mysteries.

We started across the dark field then saw another object. It was an American light tank. As we approached it, we saw that the top hatch was open.

Alongside the turret was a body. It was a GI, probably the tank commander. He was lying on his back with his legs caught up near the hatch. Where we stood on the snow, his body was just at our eye level. He was young; light snow lay on his face. We looked up at his feet and saw that they were burned off, and figured his crew was still inside the tank. We walked around the tank and kept going on our way, across the snowy fields and into the dark woods once again.

With the 1st Battalion 33rd Armored Regiment, our company took Baclain. The route to the town was filled with anti-tank fire and mortars. The 83rd Division had bypassed a German force, that later hit our F Co. hard in an ambush. Thirteen men and two officers were killed. The 83rd had not told our H.Q. that they had by-passed the enemy troops. Unfortunately, our troops thought the area was cleared.

We set up road blocks at Baclain and dug in by a road,

where we were able to relax a little bit. We brushed our teeth, ate K rations, cleaned our weapons, and slept in the foxholes. I started to clean my M1, and then was interrupted by incoming fire. I don't know exactly what it was. It might have been a few mortar shells, because they threw a lot of them at us. The Germans probably had the position zeroed in before we even arrived there.

There were a few small houses near our position, and they offered a bit of protection from the wind and cold. We could duck into them when we weren't on alert. One night I was inside talking to a few men from the squad. I think it was Plummer, Kline, and Ortolani. The rest were asleep, but we had two men outside on guard. One was Vernon Spores from Clam Falls, Wisconsin. This was the very quiet guy who smiled a lot but didn't say much. He came down the stairs to where we were in the basement and stood there. I continued talking with the men. We were probably wondering when this cold fighting would end. We talked for some time when I realized Spores was still standing there, silent.

I turned and said, "What's the matter, Spores? Is it cold out there?"

"Yes, Sergeant. But I wanted you to know that the other guy collapsed. He's lying out there in the snow."

We went out and brought him in, then sent for a medic. Apparently, he had flu or something, and was sent to the rear.

As I said, Vernon rarely talked.

Sickness, trench foot, and frost bite were big causes of the dwindling ranks of our units, but I don't remember any of my squad getting trench foot. We watched each other closely and changed our socks as often as we could. (That didn't mean that we put on new socks. We only carried one pair and wore the other. The extra socks were up inside our sweaters staying dry.)

But, some of them did get sick.

CHAPTER NINETEEN
Rations and Bandoliers

By that time the squad was made up of Roy Plummer, Rueben Kline, Carl Ortolani, Earl Cordell, Vernon Spores, and Wes Pitzer. Our driver, Charley Vories, was still with our half-track. We were all that was left. The whole company was a shadow of what it had been.

In most of the actions, the squads mixed together and fought as one unit. Our officers were there, but the only one I remember at this stage of the campaign, was "Chief" Alejandro. He had been a sergeant but got a battlefield commission in Normandy. He was Lt. "Chief" now and was platoon leader of the 3rd Platoon. We called him Chief, not lieutenant because he was an American Indian. He carried an M1 rifle like us, and he was always in the thick of the action with the squads. Chief had been hit in Soissons back in France, and had rejoined the Division, like many of us.

Boxes of K rations and cans of C rations were brought up to us, along with bandoliers of ammunition. That was a strong indication that we would be moving soon.

The indications were right. Orders came down that we were to attack two nearby towns in concert with our tanks. I learned that we were going in with Shermans, light tanks of the 1st Battalion 33rd Armor, and D Co. infantrymen of our regiment. There might have been some 83rd Division men with us. We were going to be attacking across some fields with most of the armor off to our right. They were to hit the town of Cherain while we were to go into Sterpigny.

We were to be real foot soldiers once more in this attack; no half-tracks, no tanks, just us facing the enemy. That was OK with us. By now we considered the tanks to be noisy targets for shells and machine guns, and any infantry riding the tanks were sitting ducks and the first casualties.

As the attack began, we saw the tanks starting down the hill in their sector as we walked toward a few small stone houses in our approach line. The houses appeared to be empty, and beyond them, we could see the village. In the center of it, there was a tall church steeple, and that scared us because the steeple made an excellent observation post for enemy artillery and snipers.

The deep snow slowed us down as we literally plowed ahead. Some of the D Company infantry started to bunch up, but their sergeant shouted at them and they separated. Being out in the open, in sight of the enemy, gave the soldier a natural tendency to get close to his buddies for company. But that would be a fatal move. Small bunches of soldiers were inviting targets for the enemy mortar squads.

Firing started. It was all incoming. The tanks off to our flank were taking direct fire, and we " blitz doughs" were under the indirect fire. Mortars and heavier shells slammed into the snow, leaving their usual black smudge. We ran and hit the ground, then up to run again and down, for the next group of shells. The squads started to mix together as we crossed the field. In the distance we could hear tanks burning, their ammo crackling and exploding.

I tried to guide my men toward the cover of the stone houses. We were nearly there when a particularly nasty bunch of shells came in. We heard them coming and were down flat when the blast and concussions started.

One guy dropped in front of me. He was curled up, so I could see his face. He was shaking, and his face was quivering with his eyes tightly shut. He was in a state of near panic. In that hell of a situation we were all deathly afraid, but we hung in there. We had to. Our job was to take the town up ahead. I watched the kid in front of me and thought about the expression the Southern boys in my squad used. "Ah can feel for ya, kid, but I cain't reach ya."

The shells shifted to another part of the field, and I yelled "Go for the houses!" My men jumped and ran and got inside. Reuben Klein was near a window and yelled, "Krauts!" I looked past him and there were five or six Germans running toward the village. We had our rifles up aiming out the window when a strange officer stumbled into the room. He actually had a bar on his collar. He shouted "Who's the non-com here? Who's in charge here?" We just stared at him. None of us said a word, but you could feel the silent question, "Who the hell are you?" He stared around the room, then ran out again before we could say anything. When we turned back to the window, the Krauts were long gone, and so was the strange lieutenant.

The shelling was easing up a little, so we made our exit from the house and ran toward the village. We expected rifle fire, but none came at us. To our right, I saw a Sherman coming along the road. I wondered why there was only one. We changed direction, went to the tank, and got behind it.

Then cannon fire started from the town. It had the sharp hard crack of anti-tank fire. Several shots missed our tank as it rolled off the edge of the road toward the rear of the houses in the village. Several more flat-trajectory shells came out of the town, but the tank by that time had good cover behind the houses. We figured the shell fire had to be an enemy tank.

It was. We got a quick sight of it as it changed position. It was a Panther.

The Sherman rolled across fences in the rear yards and found a gap between the houses where he could get a shot at the gray monster. He edged forward and poked his gun tube around the corner. I had my hand on our tank's hull when there was a crashing explosion and shock. A cloud of dust and debris flew all over us.

When it settled, and we could see again, the Sherman had been hit. The Panther had fired his shell straight through the wall of the house and knocked out our only tank. The crew bailed out of the Sherman and appeared to be unhurt.

From the angle of the shot, we figured that the Panther was on the other side of the street, so we decided to get over there where we could get closer to him. Then the German started to fire his bow machine gun down the street in short bursts. I suppose he was using them as warning shots, not that we needed any. We knew how dangerous he was to us. Unfortunately, we couldn't be too dangerous to him—we had no bazookas, only rifles and hand grenades.

Despite the tank's MG fire, we crossed the street in pairs, and as fast as our galoshes would carry us. Once inside the closest house, we found a small crowd of GIs, only a few of them we knew. Chief Alejandro was there; he was 3rd Platoon Leader, but I have no idea where our 1st platoon leader was. I simply can't remember if we even had one by then.

Chief had made his command post in a large house, but we didn't stay there; instead we took off on our own towards the Germans.

We were in the western end of the town, and Jerry had the eastern side. We knew they had a tank, and there must be some infantry—we saw them running toward the town from the outlying houses. So far, they hadn't shown their faces.

Our little force appeared to be parts of three E Co. squads. Sgt. Ivan Kniffen had a few men, I had some, and the third squad a few more. I think the total might have been fifteen. It was a little over a full squad. D Co. was with us, and we heard they had fourteen men left. Usually our T/O (Table of Organization) called for around sixty fighting people, not counting the officers and men at HQ.

E Co., such as it was, headed toward where we thought the Jerry tank was. Ducking through the rear of the houses, climbing into windows and knocking down doors, we arrived at the church we had seen in the distance before the attack.

The last house had an alley between it and the church. We decided to stay in this one, because it had a second story that gave us a post looking over the road. We couldn't see the tank, but if it came toward us, we knew we would be looking down into his top hatch.

I was in the alley inspecting the stone wall which surrounded the church for use as a defensive position, when someone said, "Hey Sarge, what is that?" He was pointing back to the hill that we used to enter the town. I took out my Jerry binoculars and looked at what was moving across the skyline.

"Those are Jerrys. There's a couple of half-tracks, an assault gun, more half-tracks, and they're all behind us. It looks like we're cut off—again!"

Pressing our small attack against the Panther didn't seem like a good idea anymore. How long we would be trapped in this town became a question. How much ammo did we have, how much food? How long could we last if the Krauts pressed in from the sides? Were we just cut off on the road to our rear or were we surrounded? All pressing questions that none of us could answer.

We did what we could. Guards were posted in windows and doors in whatever vantage points we could find. We figured the Panther in front of us would probably hit us first, so we looked and found gasoline in a shed. Glass bottles could be found everywhere, and we soon were busy making Molotov cocktails. They were bottles half filled with gas, then a strip of cloth was jammed into the bottle's neck as a wick. To use it, the wick was lit, and once it was flaring, the bottle was thrown at the target. When it hit and broke, the gasoline splashed and exploded. This was a good weapon against vehicles! It was all we had; no bazookas or rifle grenades. I remember we had asked for bazookas back in France. We got a nice supply of the rockets, but no launchers.

I roamed around the few houses we had in our part of the town, and got acquainted with all the rooms, doors, and passageways. Roy Plummer and Wes Pitzer were with me. Back near the C.P. we found a room with a crowd of GIs in it. They were sitting and lying around the edge of the room—doing nothing. I don't know who they were, and still don't, although I read that parts of the 83rd Division were supposed to be with our Task Force. They just sat there staring into space. What a depressing lot. We left them and moved on.

Shells started coming in, houses were hit, and some fires were started. The Panther sent some bursts of machine gun fire down the street to remind us he was still there. We went back to the house by the church where we had our Molotov cocktails ready. These were placed on the windowsills and the floors in the upper room near to the road. If Jerry rolled down on us, we would hit him from that window. That is, if he didn't have infantry giving him covering fire. We would see.

I got to know Ivan Kniffen in this action. He was 1st squad leader, but the squads rarely talked to each other. Kniffen was nearly all American Indian and appeared to most to be a surly brute. He didn't smile or try to be friendly to anyone, and he didn't like many people. Somehow, he and I had started talking and joking back at one of our assembly areas. We got along well. Under the beard and glare he was a nice guy, and I liked him. He was a good soldier.

Snow and fog joined the incoming shells. The cold was very bad. I don't know what the temperature was, but we knew it had been below freezing since the whole mess started back in December. During the day, we could heat our C or K rations with a little K ration box fire, but at night we couldn't light up unless we were in a deep basement.

Taking stock of what rations we had gave us a worrisome moment. We had made the attack with just a few rations each, expecting to be re-supplied when we took the town, but we realized that wasn't going to happen. We would have to be careful.

I was up in our room with our Molotovs, and I craned my neck out the window trying to see the Panther when I heard a voice.

"You're going to give away your position, Cullen."

Startled, I nearly fell out the window. It was Kniffen, across the street in a building that looked like a barn.

"What the hell are you doing there?" I said.

"Just looking around. There's nothing else to do. By the way, have you got any chow?"

I told him we had a few spare C ration cans, so we heaved them one at a time over to him. After the first one, the Panther fired his machine gun as if he was trying to hit each can. We were laughing like kids on a playground at each toss and burst of bullets.

Kniffen had taken a couple of his men to explore the houses just for the hell of it. He also found that this town's name was Sterpigny.

Roy, Wes, Rueben Kline, and I kept up our wandering around our part of the town. We found some of our tankers without tanks. One of them said that ten light tanks were lost in their attack. I noticed that one of the men was a pinkish-red color from head to toe. I asked him why, and he said his tank was alongside the wall of a farmhouse when a shell hit the wall. The bricks collapsed and fell on his tank and into the open hatch. He was a brick-dust soldier.

Another light tanker came up to our position by the church, then went to the stone wall at the corner of the street. He had a carbine and started to fire it at the Panther. A lot of good that did, but I guess it made him feel better.

Another tanker came up to us and asked where the Jerry was. We told him, and he started over the stone wall. We asked him where he was going, and he said he just wanted to see what was going on. Off he went, but we never saw him come back.

CHAPTER TWENTY
The Valiant Volunteer

Fog and dark didn't help our nerves or our ability to see around our perimeter. I went up to the C.P. and hung around trying to get information that I could pass on to our crew. One of the tanker boys was talking to Chief about going to find out if anyone could get through to us. He wanted to go back up the hill the way we came in, to try to establish contact with our lines. Chief agreed and told him to try it. The kid took off.

I looked into the room to check on the goldbrickers, and they were still squatting where they were before. I went back to our house by the church and told the men what was happening. Then a little after that, I went back through the houses to the C.P. area. There was a room there where I could watch for the young tanker who had volunteered for the mission.

I saw him coming out of the fog. He was staggering through the deep snow and stopped near the back of the C.P. to climb over a wire fence.

As he stopped, a shot rang out from below my window, and the kid fell and didn't move. Those lazy bastards in the room downstairs had shot him.

I felt like firing at them through the floor. I nearly

cried. That brave young tanker had been shot by some yellow bastard. What an idiot, and what a waste.

I told Chief what had happened, and then went back to my squad with Roy, Wes, Rueben, and the rest of the men. With guards on alert, we slept on the floor, stood guard, and slept again until a shot in the next room woke us up.

One of our men had been in the door facing the church alley. He had stepped back into the room for something when a huge Kraut appeared in the door. Our man fired his rifle and blew the German back out into the alley where he landed against the stone wall. He must have been six-foot five! We figured he must have been the point or scout for a probing action on our position.

I guess they got discouraged. No more appeared.

We were all getting tired and a bit hungry, although we still had some rations and found glass jars of preserved fruit in the houses.

The shelling was periodic. They would lob in four or five shells at a time, and then do nothing for half an hour or so. Then they would pick another part of the village and throw in some more. It wasn't mortar fire; it was heavy stuff. We couldn't wander around outside, so we maintained a roving patrol inside the houses.

I went back to the C.P. Chief was talking to a strange lieutenant. As they talked I crawled under a table to get some sleep, not caring that the C.P. house was burning on the upper floor.

I listened to the two officers and couldn't believe the other lieutenant was talking about surrendering. He said that we should toss in the towel or none of us would get out alive. Chief said that no, he couldn't do that. I shouted from under the table, "I'm with you Chief—no surrender!" and the unknown lieutenant walked away. I, on the other hand, went to sleep.

The hours just ran together. It was either that same night, or the next one, I can't remember, but we had some excitement.

It was getting dark outside when the Germans started an attack from the houses on the other side of the street. They started firing at our windows. It was small arms fire, and we could hear a number of separate rifles banging away—then some burp guns added their stuttering noise to the din. They were concentrating their fire in the middle of the village. I took Roy Plummer, Pitzer, Kniffen, and some others of our little band to the house where the goldbrickers were. It was the middle of our "territory." We were watching for movement, and we saw some Krauts running across the alley between the houses. I sent Roy upstairs to get a better view from a window. The German patrol continued firing from across the street, and we fired in return. We could only aim at the muzzle flashes—we couldn't see bodies.

I shot several times, and then my rifle jammed. I hadn't cleaned it properly since the last action, and now I couldn't get the spent cartridge case out of the breech. The extractor had torn off the rim of the jammed shell.

I got away from the window and tried using a knife to pry it out—no good. Then I ran into the room with the sitting GIs and begged for a rifle. They wouldn't even look up at me.

"One of you guys give me a weapon! Give me a gun, come on," I shouted.

But none of them made a move. I was afraid to grab one, for fear they would shoot me. I ran back to the hallway and was standing in the open door when someone shouted, "They're setting up a machine gun."

Realizing I was out in the open, I started to move away towards the cover of thick stone walls when a voice behind me said, "What's going on here?"

I turned sideways to answer him when a stream of green tracers came ripping under my chin and hit the guy in the chest. It was a Lieutenant, I guess, from the immobile group in the back room.

He didn't know it, but he had saved my life. More

tracers and bullets came cracking across the room. I ducked under it and went to the officer who was lying on his back. Someone put a flashlight on him, and he was turning green already. We dragged him out of the way. Then I took his .45 pistol since I figured he wouldn't need it anymore and I needed a weapon. I went back to the side of the door, and then the stream of bullets stopped. The few of us there waited for a rush of Germans, when Roy Plummer came running down the stairs. "I got him, Jim. I got him."

He had seen the German machine gun from his position and had picked him off. That stopped the attack, and all was quiet again.

On guard a bit later by our church wall, I heard the squeaking rumble of a tank. I thought it was our friend, the Panther, but after a period of panic, I learned it was our own tanks with the 83rd Division, who had broken through to us. We were relieved of the position.

We got ready to leave Sterpigny. The Panther tank was left to another task force, Task Force Richardson we later learned, and they took care of it. . They outflanked the town, came in from the east, and hit our Panther in the rear as he started to run. The shell that hit the German stopped it right in front of our alley by the church's stone wall.

CHAPTER TWENTY ONE
Just Doing A Job

It was a short march to the next town. A roadside sign said Cherain. The town looked just like Sterpigny, with small stone houses clustered near a single road with hills at the edge of town. We didn't get a chance to go into the village. Instead our company was directed to a hill at the edge of town. Then we were told that Task Force Lovelady had tried twice to take the hill and had been beaten back each time. We were the lucky ones for the third try.

Picking up some rations, we spread out to start up the slope. I was shocked at the size of the company. What happened to everybody? We looked like an understaffed platoon, not a company.

The signal came, and the line started up. Each step in the snow that carried us higher brought the thought that a Jerry machine gun would start any minute. We expected the shells to start, too. But our line went up and up, closer to the tree line, and still nothing happened. Then we thought the Krauts would wait until we were near the trees; exhausted from the climb in two- foot-deep snow, then it would start! But it didn't. We got into the blessed cover of the trees, and the only sound was our own wheezing breath.

Orders came up to "dig in along the tree line," so we did. Getting through the snow was easy; breaking into the frozen ground was not. But hard ground or not, we were soon working as hard as we could to dig because Jerry finally started throwing in some big shells. Some were aimed at the village and some at us on the hill. Kniffen and I dug a two-man hole just as fast as we could, then I checked on what was left of my squad. They were all dug in deep enough.

Jerry started some serious shelling on our position, and then switched to mortars for a while. We stayed in the holes and waited, but there were no infantry attacks after the barrage. Chief was moving back and forth checking on our line, and then he'd flop down near us and talk to the CP on his sound-powered phone. I asked him what was happening and why we were up here.

He replied ,"We'll be going through the woods into the attack again, but I don't know when."

"What will we be attacking?"

"The next town," he said.

Oh well.

Back in my foxhole, Kniffen and I talked about the last action we had gone through. We knew we were beating the hell out of the Krauts, but this fighting in Sterpigny, and now Cherain, didn't prove that. Jerry was fighting back and hurting us. Didn't he know when to quit? A lot of our tanks were destroyed in those two towns, but we didn't know what damage we had done to his forces. It's always true, unfortunately, that the attacker will lose more than the defender if the defender is well positioned.

More shelling started. We sat at the edge of the hole listening and watching. We were both old hands now, well experienced in the sounds of the battlefield. We could catch the distant whisper of an H.E. shell, follow it by ear, and know where it would land. Some shells came over and we didn't move. We knew they were going to hit at the far end of the hill. We were at the stage in combat experience where perhaps we knew too much and were getting over-confident. It wasn't bravery or fearlessness; it just bordered on carelessness. We were giving ourselves too wide a margin. Also, we were bone tired and worn out. Some people called it the numbness of too much combat.

We had been in combat here in the Ardennes since December 20 when we entered the campaign in Trois Ponts. We had been in contact with the enemy every day, except for a couple of days out of the line getting ready for the next battle.

Before the Ardennes, our regiment had fought all the way from Normandy to Germany with very little rest. In contact with the enemy, it was a seven-day workweek, and here in the Ardennes, the nights were included. Not only was our 36th Armored Regiment worn and beat up; it was the whole 3rd Armored Division. Casualties were high not only in men, but in equipment. We all were exhausted.

We heard voices and saw two officers coming up the hill. They stopped near our hole. I saw that one of them was British. I recognized their battle dress. The other, I think, was one of our majors. They chatted for a few minutes, and then the Briton shook hands with the major, turned and went off into the woods. As he left, I asked our officer who that was.

"Oh, just someone who is doing a job for us." He turned and went back down the hill.

Years later I asked some more questions about the British officer and learned that he was probably one of British General Montgomery's Phantom Group. He sent them out to the front lines to report directly to him all the latest intelligence.

"Let's go," Chief shouted. We picked up our gear and strapped it on. We had a web belt with a canteen and a medic pouch, a musette bag with rations, a bandolier of rifle ammo, and our rifles. We started forward into the woods.

We tried to duck the branches with the heavy snow burden, but there was always one ready to pile down our necks. My helmet caught on a twig and I stopped and bent over to free it.

An explosion blasted right in front of me, and my legs were knocked out from under me. It felt like a pick or a sledgehammer had been swung at my leg. I was face down in the snow, cursing, swearing, and screaming with my teeth clenched tightly together. I was angry more than hurt—angry that those bastards had hit me again. God damn them! I said it over, and over again—those lousy bastards.

The mortar shells kept coming in, and thankfully there were no tree bursts. I tried to move, and then felt myself getting dragged toward a foxhole. It was Roy Plummer and Pitzer. They were as low as they could crouch and still pull me toward the hole.

Finally, we tumbled in and I looked down at my right leg, surprised to see that it was still there. Steam was rising from the blood that was pouring onto the ice at the bottom of the foxhole. The leg hurt, but not that much. I just felt shocked and numb.

Roy opened my medic pack and poured the sulfa powder on the open wound in my leg, then tried to give me water for the pills that were in the pack. He pulled at his canteen trying to get it out of its cover, then muttered that he couldn't get it out. He half turned, and I said, "Roy, you won't get that canteen out, ever. It's shot full of holes."

The mortar shell that got me had sent several pieces of metal through Roy's canteen. It was a sieve, and Roy was a very lucky man.

We pulled out my canteen; the water was slushy ice, but we got the pills into me. All the time the calls were going out for "Medic! Medic!" Rueben Kline had a bad hit in his shoulder from the same shell, and I think Cordell got hit also, and we weren't even bunched up.

The Medic came; Roy and the men patted me on the helmet and said goodbye. They went off to continue the attack, and the medics took us all down the hill. I don't remember being carried down to the village, but somehow, they got us into a room in a house. Jerry was still shelling, and I lay on a stretcher and swore at him.

From the village of Cherain, ambulances took us back to a receiving station. It was in a big church. We wounded GIs were on stretchers on the floor near the altar. It was cold, and I kept getting colder and colder.

An orderly went past me, and I asked him for another blanket. He got me one right away, but it didn't seem to help. I was freezing. The Medic came back after a while and asked how I was doing, and I told him I was cold.

Someone else looked at me and at my leg, and then they started pumping blood into my arm. They had a hell of a time finding a vein, but when they did, I started to get warm again. It was a great feeling as the heat spread throughout my whole body.

From the church, there was another trip farther back to a hospital where they operated on my leg and took out, I guess, the bits and pieces of my uniform and odd chunks of metal. The shrapnel, I was told, went right through my leg in between the two bones, severing the nerve to the foot and leaving it numb forever. "Very lucky," they said, and I agreed.

CHAPTER TWENTY TWO
All The Luck

In a Paris hospital, I realized my leg hadn't been stitched up yet when I saw the wound one day. The nurses were changing the dressings and bandages when I looked down and saw the gaping hole in my leg. I guess they were still opening and cleaning the wound, watching for infection. Eventually I was taken to an operating room and stitches were put in.

Mail still arrived in bunches, and each letter was a treat. I loved all the news about my brother, Martin, and his flying in the Air Corps. He had been drafted originally into the Quartermaster Corps and then transferred to the Air Corps as an air cadet. Now he was training in B-24s and getting ready to fly to the Pacific. Several letters told me about a leave he had from the Army at Christmas. One letter from Dad said that Martin set up our electric trains, and he and Billy, our younger brother, had a great time. There was news about all our old friends, Ed Reiss, Jack Hogan, Dick Burns, Warren Poling, Fred Elbrecht, and the rest. All of them were scattered around the world in the service.

I wrote home and sent letters to my outfit still fighting in Germany. Then one letter came from Roy Plummer.

Germany
Feb. 7, 45
Hi Jim—

I received you letter today and was sure glad to hear from you.

Glad to hear you got back O.K. and all is going fine, I sure hope all works out O.K. and your leg gets perfectly well. I was glad to know you had seen Kline and I sure hope he makes it through O.K. I sure hope he doesn't lose his arm.

I am taking care of your stuff and will have it mailed right away. C.O. is on pass and will be back tomorrow so will get the P38 and send it. The C.O. said it would be O.K. to send it in the mail. So I sure hope you get it and the rest of your things.

You are a Staff, so don't worry any more about that. I haven't got a knife anymore but will see if any other of the boys have one.

Well kid here is the dope since you left us.

After you got hit I went down in the woods and dug in. We stayed there that day & night, and did It ever rain and snow. Anyway Pitzer and I got a pass to Paris the next morning. Can you imagine that. The Jerrys were still shelling us a lot, and plenty of mortar. It was about 8:00 o'clock when we left our foxhole and went down the hill again to Battalion & from there to Regt. & on to Paris. Was we ever glad to get out of that mess. There were 10 men and one officer left in the company when it was relieved. And the company was relieved the same day we went to Paris.

Anyhow I had a swell time in Paris. And the trip took 7 days altogether. When I came back to the outfit they were in Mean, Belgium. And all new men and up to strength again.

Us fellows that went through all the mess are getting the bronze star. 11 men altogether. I sure wish you could have made it to.

Here we are back in Germany & plenty of rest & good food. But you can guess what we are going to be doing soon.

Kniffen has the second sg. now & I still have the 1st. All the old men are O.K. (The few that are left)

I sure will be glad to hear from you anytime Jim, so write once in a while.

Your friend,
Roy P.

I felt sorry for the men, but happy that Roy now had a squad. I knew he could make a good leader. He was calm and steady, and he didn't panic in action. I missed him and Wes Pitzer, but not enough to want to go back up where they were. It was okay the first time I rejoined the Company and went back into combat, but I figured by now I had used up my luck.

Of course, if I were ordered back into the line—I would go, but I also thought that my leg wound would put me in the "limited duty" category. An infantryman needs two good legs, and so far, I only had one.

More mail came in—all out of sequence, and this time I was shocked at a letter from my mother saying that Connie was "expecting."

Connie was my brother's *girlfriend,* and my mother seemed to be happy about it. This I didn't understand, because my mother was more Victorian in her beliefs than the Queen herself.

Several days later, a new bundle of letters told me that Martin and Connie were married in Seymour, Indiana, when he got his wings. Mom, Dad, and Billy went by train and nearly collapsed from the Midwest heat and humidity. So, all was well at home.

Once my leg was stitched up I was able to move around on crutches, although standing up straight hurt quite a bit. I suppose it was from the blood finding new paths—or something like that. However, that didn't stop me from going down to the courtyard to see Fred Astaire, the great dancer and movie star. He did some snappy tap dancing and sang many of his songs from the movies. At the end of one dance bit, he made us howl with laughter when he took off his toupee and fanned his sweating brow with it. What a hit! He was the only "star entertainer" I saw when I was overseas.

I progressed in my walking as the pain decreased, and I learned to really fly with the crutches. I was dismissed from the hospital, and by ambulance, was taken to a recuperation center somewhere in France. It was in a tent city, made up of many tents, each holding ten or twelve beds.Back in Paris, I had enjoyed a single room with peace and quiet. Now I shared a tent with eleven other guys who cried, snored at night, and kept yelling for codeine. Other than that, they were OK—just normal GIs waiting to heal.

During the day we talked back and forth from our beds, and it appeared that we were all leg cases. Insults were traded about hometowns and Army units. The soldier from the 30th Division was told his Division was named the "Brassiere Boys" because they "contained Brest," the city on the French coast that the Germans refused to surrender until September 18, 1944. Despite it all, we were a comparatively happy little group because we were out of the miserable winter fighting and in warm, soft beds.

One day a medical officer came into our ward and examined each GI. He looked at my chart and my leg, and then said, "OK. You're OK for going back to duty."

I asked, "How am I going to do that? I can't even walk."

He told me, "Get out of bed and stand up."

I did, and he saw that I couldn't bend my right ankle. Not saying a word, he left, and I got back into bed. The other GIs in the ward all agreed that the doctor was a bit of a jerk. He had already given the same treatment to some of them in the ward. Maybe, we thought, they are trying to clear the ward for the new casualties.

The next morning some orderlies came to my bed and said, "Say goodbye to your buddies. You're out of here."

I asked if I was going back to the Division, and they said, "No, you're bound for England."

Well, that was great news. England was a long way from the front lines!

Several of us were taken to Le Havre by ambulance and carried aboard a white hospital ship. As the ship approached the English Coast, I hobbled over to a porthole to see the White Cliffs of Dover gleaming in the sun. What a beautiful sight.

At the new hospital, they labored to get my ankle working again, and they did a good job. I had been hit on January 18th, and now, at the end of March 1945, I could walk. While I was in the rehab hospital, Jack Hogan, an old friend from Brooklyn, got my address from home, and came to visit. He took some pictures and sent them home to my folks with a reassuring letter. Jack was in the Air Force with the 352 Fighter Squadron 353 Fighter Group.

(S/Sgt Cullen in hospital in England.)

The rehab hospital finished their work, and then sent me to another rehab camp where we were back in tents. This place was designed to wake up our flabby muscles and to exercise every part of our GI bodies. It was painful. The first several days of calisthenics, running, and pushups were terrible. All those weeks of lying in bed had really softened us up. Our muscles screamed in pain when our rehab platoon staggered into the tents at the end of each day. The pain finally went away, though, and we slowly got back into shape.

I got a "delay en route" when I was discharged from the hospital. That gave me ten days to go to Raydon Airfield to see Jack Hogan, and then to Scotland to see my grandparents before I reported to a new post.

Busses and trains took me to both places, and I had a wonderful time. At the airbase, I was up close to the squadron's P-51 fighters and had some pictures taken. One flight came back from a mission while we were standing near the runway, and it was great to see the planes peel off, one by one, and pop their landing gear as they made their sweep across the field.

I then went to London and caught a train to Glasgow. On the way I met a man, a civilian, who worked for Remington, a U.S. company. He was a Scot. When we arrived in Glasgow, it was late in the evening and no busses were running, so he took me to meet his family, gave me dinner, and a place to sleep. The next morning, I caught a bus for Renton.

(S/Sgt Cullen while visiting family in Scotland after discharge
from hospital.)

I had been to Renton in 1937 with Billy and my
mother, so it was not a strange town. Granny McLean,
Mom's mother who had remarried, hadn't changed much.
She was quiet and calm, and a very nice person—like the
"Mater" which is what we called my Mother. Relatives

came in, and I remembered some and didn't know others. It was hectic until I went to Alexandria to my other grandparents—Dad's parents. Both were short and cheery. Again, more relatives and family friends were there. This time I met my cousins and Dad's brothers and sisters. I took cousin Agnes Waters to Glasgow for lunch, and we had a great time. She introduced me to that German song, "Lilli Marlene." I had never heard it before.

The next day I was walking down the street in Alexandria when a woman came over to me. I thought she was going to say, "You're Meg Kelso's son, aren't you?"

However, she instead said, "I'm awfully sorry to hear about your President."

When I asked what happened, she said, "He just died."

Now that was a shock. I really felt terrible that Roosevelt was gone; he was our leader and Commander-in-Chief.

In retrospect, I actually can't remember a lot of detail about my visit to Scotland. It was all one big blur of handshakes, hugs, and kisses.

I made my way back to England, reported to a base, and then boarded a ship to return to France. All the GIs on the ship were combat wounded and no doubt headed for "limited duty." That meant no more front-line combat for us.

I buddied up with a stocky guy named Hec Kilrea, who happened to be Canadian. He was also a S/Sgt. and a gentleman, always smiling and cheery. I soon learned Kilrea loved to drink. When we landed in France, we were trucked to a railhead and were piled into French freight cars—the famous 40 x 8 of WWI:—forty men or eight horses.

The train didn't exactly fly across France. It was stop and go, with more "stops" than "gos". At one long wait in an unknown location, some of the men left the train and went into town. Kilrea went with them. They had been gone a few hours when the engine whistled and tooted, then started to move. The men from our box car came running across the rail yard. I saw Kilrea; he was running with two bottles in his hands. Running across railroad tracks and ties isn't easy, especially when you've been drinking—and it was evident that he had been. The train was moving and picking up speed when he got close to our door. We reached out to grab him while we yelled, "Faster! Faster!" We couldn't catch his hands because of the bottles. Finally, he made a lunge, dropped one of his bottles, and I caught his hand. After a struggle, we pulled him aboard. He was laughing and giggling; definitely drunk.

CHAPTER TWENTY THREE
Extraordinary Experiences

We were trucked from the rail yard in big, open trucks to Granville, France, our final stop, . on the Brittany Coast. For fun, along the way at crossroads, where Military Police were on duty, we shouted, "M.P.s eat shit!" as we rode past. Then when we reached Granville, we found that we were going to be assigned to a Military Police Battalion! "We" were now "them"! Talk about humiliating!

It turned out that being M.P.s wasn't that bad. We lived in a large, three-story apartment in the new part of town, and Kilrea was my roommate. The outfit was the 387th Military Police Battalion, "B" Company. Our room had double bunks and I chose the top one. There was a sink in the room, but the toilet was down the hall. It was a comfortable life compared to the front lines. There was a large mess hall nearby, and we learned it was set up when Gen. Eisenhower had his H.Q. in Granville.

After we settled in, we were issued a .45 automatic pistol, white helmet liner, white pistol belts, white leggings, and an M.P. armband. All the gear said we were Military Police, but underneath we were still infantrymen. I thought, *Here we go again with on-the-job training*. We knew how to handle a weapon, but handling traffic was a mystery.

Our job turned out to be very easy. We patrolled the streets, bars, and whorehouses, and tried to keep other GIs out of trouble. The "cat houses" were designated Off Limits, and so were many of the bars. That meant that U.S. soldiers were not to go near these places, though many of them tried.

During my time with the 3rd Armored, most of us were in the 18 to 20 age group, and we came from a society that did not discuss sex. Films were censored, books were "banned" in Boston, and anything to do with sex was whispered. I would guess that nearly all the GIs in our platoon, even our Company, were pretty ignorant of the ways of the world.

None of my squad was married, and the subject of sex rarely came up. Sex was probably the last thing on our minds when we were on the line. When we took the towns in France and Belgium, we were surrounded by pretty girls whenever the column stopped. We got hugs and kisses, and that was the end of it. There were too many other things to worry and think about—survival being the most pressing one.

I had a platoon with my own jeep and driver. Our patrols covered that part of Granville that was our territory. We had some of the new city, and the entire "old city" which was centuries old and embraced the harbor. Life was comparatively easy.

I look back at my duty in the Military Police and recall that that was my first close look at sex in the French manner. In Granville, in particular, our platoon had to inspect the local "houses" in the old part of town. By old, I mean centuries old with narrow, crooked cobblestone streets that wound between the ancient houses. We were charged with making sure the "houses" were off limits to all allied soldiers. We knew each parlor and got to know the people who worked there. The girls were usually farm girls who spent a few years at the trade, and then went back to the farm with a pocketful of money. Each had to have a "carnet sanitaire" meaning a health certificate from the city doctor. They were given health examinations once a month.

The house usually had a parlor on the ground floor where everyone gathered in the evening. Wine was the drink of choice. The customers sat and talked, smoking and sipping wine. They talked to each other and the girls— it was very pleasant. Some men would go upstairs with a girl, others didn't. For those that didn't, it was like an English pub.

The house owners were happy to see us MPs because we gave them protection from any drunken GI. The girls were happy to see us because they liked to tease us. They would ask us to "zig zig" and we would shake our heads and say, "non." They knew that we couldn't do that deed. They would laugh and point to our helmets, white with MP on the front. They called us Maquereau Professionel, or fish peddlers. I understand that meant pimp in French. They were kidding us. I think.

My roommate, Hec Kilrea, was still trying to drink up all the Calvados and wine in France. He was pretty good at his attempts, and he was still a good buddy—happy and jovial at all times, even pissed to the gills. One day one of my men brought me a copy of the Stars and Stripes and showed me a notice about a GI getting the D.S.C. medal— the Distinguished Service Cross. He said, "Is this Sgt. Kilrea?" It was a story about the awarding of the honor to a S/Sgt. Hec Kilrea, a great ice hockey player with the Toronto Maple Leafs.

(S/Sgt Cullen with Hec Kilrea in Granville, France.)

I found Hec and showed him the article. "Yeah. That was a day that I was particularly stupid. I lost my front false teeth doing that." That's all he said about the D.S.C.

He was a great guy, but I never did find out from him what he did to earn the medal. The Stars and Stripes article said that he knocked out two German tanks.

After a few months, my platoon was transferred to Le Mans, but Hec Kilrea and the other platoon were transferred to another town, and I never saw them again.

While at Le Mans I learned that the personal effects of many wounded soldiers were shipped to a depot near Paris. I got a pass to go there and retrieve whatever I could find for my outfit. The effects were packed into 60-mm mortar shell containers. These were strong cardboard tubes about a foot and a half long with metal caps on the ends. When I got back, the men were happy to get their wallets and letters and cigarette lighters they thought were "long gone."

Then I got another pass to Paris to see my old friend, Dick Burns, now a 1st Lt. This time I had to hitch a ride on a truck. Once there, Dick showed me the highlights of the town, and we had a great time for two days and nights.

When I got back to Le Mans, the platoon was detailed for two extraordinary experiences. The first was guard duty at the execution of an American soldier who had been convicted in the rape and murder of a young French girl. He had committed the crime in an old quarry, and that's where he was going to be executed by hanging. Apparently, the Army policy was to bring the portable hanging platform to the original scene of the crime. We went by truck to the quarry, and then set up a perimeter guard.

At the appointed time, 6 x 6 trucks arrived with the prisoner and the escort. He was a young GI from "the rear echelon".

Our orders were to do an about face when he was put on the platform, and I shouted the command at the appropriate time. We then heard the bang of the platform, and the deed was done. The platoon assembled, climbed into our trucks, and left the area.

A few weeks later we got the call again. This time it was a rape only case, but the verdict was guilty, and the sentence was execution by hanging. The chief executioner for the E.T.O. was John C. Woods. He was a short, heavy guy, and I had met him at the first hanging, when he told us the drill - what to do and where to stand. This time he came into town early and we had a few drinks together. He said that he had "dropped" nearly a hundred GIs, and like the one this time, most were members of the rear echelon. All were for rape, or murder, or both. This time the hanging would be in the farmyard of the house where the rape took place. I noted that he always carried a .45 automatic on his hip. He said, "All of these guys have buddies, and I'm not taking a chance."

On the day of the hanging, he gave us our timetable and routine, and we were trucked to the site. The perimeter was set up and then the prisoner arrived. Just before we did our "about face", I saw the young farm girl whom I assumed was the victim, peeking around the corner of the farmhouse. She took a quick look and then disappeared. We stood at parade rest—then heard the bang of the "drop."

Later I learned that 140 soldiers had been executed in the E.T.O.

On one occasion, our little detachment was invited to the town of Évreux. They wanted us to drive into town in our jeeps at exactly three in the afternoon in a repetition of their liberation the year before by a unit of the 1st Army. After we rode in, our small column was toasted and praised in the village square. Then a banquet started at seven PM and lasted until after midnight. Seated next to each of us was a pretty mademoiselle. We had a great time.

Chartres was our next post, but only briefly. As it happened, Germany surrendered while we were there.

Hec Kilrea had been transferred out back in Granville, and we could have used his knowledge of drinking in our celebration of V.E. day. Thanking God that we had lived through the war, several of us toured all the bars in Chartres. Early in the dawn we managed to get back to the barracks, which was a block away from the cathedral. We drank some water from a spigot in the wall. The water got us going again—the buzz came back, and we went back downtown. We were a very happy bunch.

A few days later orders put us on the road again. This time we were going to Caen, a city to the north. Only five of us went there; the rest of the platoon was transferred elsewhere.

The "point system" was announced. Each soldier was given a certain number of points for a variety of things: married, children, years in service, wounds, and so forth. Each category added to the total. If you had 85 points, you were put at the top of the list to go home.

I came up with 78. Not too bad, but I would have to wait a bit longer for my turn.

Coming into Caen, we were surprised at the destruction. The city had been bombed by the Canadians and British just before our breakout from Normandy. Gen. "Monty" Montgomery, the British commander, had ordered the bombing to aid his last attack. He had battered away at the gates of Caen since D-Day, but with little success. The final bombing had obliterated most of the city – thirty thousand civilians along with the German troops.

Monty had proclaimed the capture of Caen as a D-Day objective. It fell on July 9th, 1944.

At the Military Police headquarters in Caen, I met the Lt. who was Provost Marshal. His name escapes me, but he was pretty good. S/Sgt. Blaine Sterner was the Detachment Sergeant, and I reported to him. There were about forty to fifty men in our unit—all typical GIs. All had seen combat, and they were all anxious to go home.

Routine patrols of the city streets occupied our time. In between, the men loafed, drank downtown in the bars that had survived, wrote home, and played baseball. There was an open field nearby where they chose up sides for games.

We had a small dining room and ate in shifts. German prisoners of war waited on us and did the cleaning. They also did laundry. Four or five of them, still in German uniforms with a "P" on the backs, were trucked in every morning and back to their camp every night. As usual, these prisoners were very happy to be where they were, instead of a Russian POW camp.

We got the same prisoners every day, so we got to know them pretty well. One was a craftsman who carved wood objects for us. For a couple packs of cigarettes, he made a mahogany picture frame for me. Where he got the wood, I never asked.

Our C.O. was a blustery loud talker, but a nice guy. His bark was strong, but he didn't mean it.

One night we got a call concerning a truck full of anti-tank mines that had exploded over near Bayeux. They wanted an American to OK some papers. The C.O. and I drove over in his jeep, and when we arrived at the site, we were taken to a large crater where the truck had exploded. Twenty Frenchmen were on the truck when something happened, and the German Teller mines they were loading exploded. In the explosion, the truck and the men just disappeared—nothing was left.

My C.O. had to go with some of the French officials and he said, "Sgt., take the jeep over to the houses at the edge of the field, and I'll meet you there." I said, "Sir, I can't drive." He exploded like the truck.

"What do you mean, you can't drive? Everybody can drive. I've never heard of a Yank that can't drive." He went on for five minutes at full blast.

Finally, I saluted, climbed into the jeep, and with a great grinding of gears, drove off. Sure, I had driven, but not much before the war, and I didn't get a license until 1947. When we met later, he never said a word, but he took the wheel back to Caen.

The C.O. was also in on the end of a nasty episode; one that endeared him to me. We had one soldier who was a solid pain in the ass. During the day he was quiet and placid and didn't talk much. At night, on leave, he would hit the Calvados and go crazy. One night he staggered back to the barracks with the front of his uniform all bloody. I had him taken to the medics and later heard his story.

He had been drinking and was approached by a prostitute. He had tried to take her on right then and there. In his drunken state, he tried to do the deed on the ground, missed the target, and jammed his dick into the gravel on the road. He tore a gash in his member, and the medics sewed him up.

He had recovered from that, when a few weeks later he went out drinking again. This time he attacked a civilian Frenchman after many drinks. The Frenchman called us, and I sent a patrol to pick up our drunken friend, and they hauled him in. He bunked on the top floor of the building, and I went up there to talk to him. The patrol had told me that he had hit the Frenchman because he had "breathed loudly" as he passed.

Our man, I'll call him Ralph, was in bed when I entered the room. He made some smart-ass, drunken remarks about Frenchmen when I questioned him. Then I started to tell him what I thought about him as a soldier. He said I wouldn't say that if I didn't have stripes on my arm. He offered to beat me up if I'd take them off.

I took him up on the offer. Stupidly, though, I didn't keep my eye on him as I took off my shirt. He hit me over the eye with a big, swinging punch. I got my arm out of the shirt, and we went at it. It wasn't a long fight, but it ended when I had him against the wall, putting punches into his chest and stomach. Then he collapsed on the floor. I told the Corporal that was with me to take care of him, and I left. A little later I heard that he woke up and complained about his side. They took him to the medics and found three broken ribs.

The next afternoon, the C.O. called me in. I expected a court-martial was coming up for me. Fighting in the ranks was bad, but a Sgt. hitting a Pvt. was very bad. He looked at me when I reported to him, then he smiled and said, and "Did you hit a door knob with that eye, Sergeant?" I said,

"It was something like that, Sir."

Then he noted that "Our boy is in the hospital again, I see. I think I will see about a transfer for him. This duty is too rough for him. Do you agree?"

I agreed, and I never heard another word about it. That he knew all about the episode, I had no doubt. He could have put me up on charges, but he didn't.

A few weeks later Ralph was transferred to another Battalion. Then Tech Sgt. Blaine Sterner went home on Points, and I became Detachment Sergeant. Our Commanding Officer was transferred, and a new C.O. came to our unit—1st Lt. John Scioli. He turned out to be a very good officer. He came from Philadelphia, and we got along well.

Somehow, Lt. Scioli commandeered a 1935 Ford sedan. I don't know how he got it, but he used it as his command car, and I would occasionally do patrols in the "limousine." It was much better than riding in the open jeep I was usually in. I also had a driver, Corp. Gibson, a wisecracking Irishman—I think from Brooklyn.

The weeks passed with everyone waiting for their Points number to come up. But the wait wasn't boring. We were called to go out one rainy night for a truck accident. A soldier telephoned us that the truck he was in had overturned in the fog, when it went off the road. He said there was a driver, but he couldn't find him. I took four men and a 6 x 6 truck and went to the accident scene. We found the truck, also a 6 x 6, but not the driver.

Putting a cable onto the truck that was lying on its side, we pulled it upright and found the driver. He was face down in the ditch. The running board of the truck had speared him in the back. Before we loaded him into the back of our vehicle, we went through his pockets and found a note that showed he had the magic number—85 points.

A couple of nights later, the radio alerted us to two AWOL soldiers who were in our area. They were not smart. In making their getaway, they stole an ambulance. This vehicle had huge red crosses on all sides—even on the roof. My driver and I, and two other jeeps went out searching, then got word that an ambulance was seen in Bayeaux. We went there, searched a few streets, and caught them. They had parked the marked vehicle on the street when they went in to visit their girlfriends.

For fun, we drove up north to Ouistreham on the coast where they had some nice bars. We also went to Cherbourg, but Ouistreham was our favorite. In the bistro on the shore, we met and made friends with a young girl and her mother. We could talk and dance with her and have a glass of wine, but Mother was never far away.

Time passed and more and more of our unit were "redeployed" back to the States. Finally, my number came up. I said goodbye to the detachment and wished them all well. I was going home to Mom, Dad, and Billy. My other brother, Martin, was on his way to the Pacific as a B-24 pilot. He was married and had a baby on the way, and his wife, Connie, was all alone except for both sets of parents who lived nearby.

The Army set up several tent cities near the port city of Le Havre to house the troops that were heading home. They were called the "Cigarette Camps". They were named "Old Gold," "Lucky Strike," "Chesterfield," and so on. I drew "Lucky Strike."

It was a short truck ride to Le Havre from Caen. On the way, the truck picked up additional GIs and I noticed that everyone had a smile on his face. The war was over, and we were going home!

The tents were the usual pyramidal canvas types that slept four or five men. We settled in with a lot of laughs and jokes. Everyone was feeling good.

This didn't last long, however. I suppose we expected too much. We had visions of an overnight stay in the camp, then a quick boarding on a luxury liner, and then off to the States. That did not happen.

After the first three days, we knew we were in for a bit of a wait. We learned that we were in one of nine huge camps that were tent cities. There were movie theatres, chapels, PXs, laundries, baseball fields, and hospitals—everything a huge mob of GIs needed.

As far as my little tent was concerned, we needed none of it. We wanted out. A large part of our feelings, no doubt, resulted from the fact that we were not part of a unit. We had no identity other than being U.S. soldiers. We each wore our old Division's patch on our right shoulder, proudly, but we had no "home" base.

We waited, bored and restless. We knew from the size of the tent cities, that many ships would be needed to carry all of us home. We also knew the Army was doing a big job in this redeployment, but we were not impressed.

Inspirational meetings were called to keep up our spirits. Large groups of GIs would be called from the tents and assembled in one large tent. Officers from the

Quartermaster Corps or Service of Supply gave speeches. They would tell us about the great job we had done and why there were no ships at the dock for us. When the crowd couldn't take any more of the BS, some GI would shout "48". From the opposite side of the tent another GI would answer "49" real loud. Then from the back came the yell, "50" and the whole tent full of men would scream at the top of their lungs, "Soooooooom shit." Then everyone collapsed laughing. Everyone, that is, except the officers.

After the pep talks, back we went to the tents and waited. At times the men said it was worse than combat because nothing was happening, and we didn't have a job or a mission, just the hope of a ship coming to bring us home.

The wait was probably just a few weeks, but it seemed forever. The weather made it worse because we were into December, and it was cold, rainy, and miserable.

CHAPTER TWENTY FOUR
You're Not in France Anymore!

All that disappeared one day when we were called out for another formation. These "company" formations were not the usual "Dress right, dress—Ready, front" type of line up. We just stood there in a rough three-man line while a couple of Sergeants and an officer would stand in front and read announcements on our conduct and coming events, the most important of which was who was shipping out.

Glory be! A few of us in my tent were called out. We were going home! It was true—the Sergeant in charge handed us the written orders and told us to pack. We were going the next day.

Early the next morning we went to the end of our "company street" and were trucked to a dock in Le Havre. We boarded a smaller ship than I came over on. It was the "Dominican Victory" which was a freighter a wee bit longer than a Liberty ship. As usual, our bunks were down in the hold where freight was carried. It was the lowest part of the ship, but we didn't really care—it was on a ship that was headed west.

It was a rough winter crossing. Huge grey seas rolled past us when we were up on deck, and the ship pitched and rolled with them. When the bow went down into a wave, the propeller came out of the water vibrating the whole ship. The rattling and shaking didn't worry us though—we were going home.

Six or seven days later we sailed into New York Harbor and docked at a pier in Manhattan. My letter had arrived before me, and there was my father waiting on the dock. Since he worked on ships in the Harbor, he had a Coast Guard pass to go wherever he wanted. It was great to see him, even though we only had a minute or two together before we were put on an Army bus for Ft. Dix, NJ. Years later, he told me he had watched the way I walked to see if I had a limp.

Getting discharged wasn't too bad. It took a quick physical, a bunch of paperwork, and some waiting around doing nothing. The night we arrived at Dix, several of us went to the PX for snacks. They had cold, fresh milk at the counter, and we couldn't get enough. We all gulped down several bottles. It was the first time we had had real milk in a long time.

On the way back to the barracks, a couple of the men stopped in the middle of the road to pee. It was dark, around 8 o'clock, and the men weren't giving what they were doing a second thought. Then one of the guys shouted, "Hey, what are you doing? You're in the States now—you're not in France anymore."

We all laughed and went to the barracks to sleep.

In the United States after we were discharged, the great American armies were absorbed into the stream of a peace-time society. WW II was put on the shelf. Most GIs didn't give the biggest war in history much thought. They were too busy working, going to school, and raising families. Some men joined the veterans' groups and relived their great adventure in talks with other veterans. Not too many war stories were told to families, and in most cases, the families never asked questions. The war was in the past. We were home.

CHAPTER TWENTY FIVE
Just Like the Army

The past sixty plus years have been good to me and I have been extremely lucky, just like in combat. After the Army said goodbye, I waited at home, doing nothing except greeting my friends who came home one after another as their points gave them a pass.

Dick Burns came home from Paris. Jack Hogan came from England. My brother, Martin, came home from Japan. Eddie Reiss came home from California, and the others arrived in good time.

For one week I worked for a phony check writer service company. I knew it was a bad company when a "customer" threatened to hit me but wouldn't because he saw my "ruptured duck", my discharge pin, on my lapel. Then I did some office work at Benjamin Moore Co. in lower Manhattan. It was, and still is, a paint company and a very good one, but I didn't care for the deskwork.

Dick Burns, at this point, suggested that we both apply to college. The GI Bill was in effect, and a new college system was being set up in New York State. It was the Associated Colleges of Upper N.Y. State. Classes started in old military camps, with teachers and professors drafted from all the major N.Y. schools. We applied for and were accepted at Champlain College. It was in the old Plattsburg Barracks on Lake Champlain.

It was like being back in the Army. All the students were veterans, and we all got along well. Everyone was well-disciplined and deadly serious about study, and it was a good time.

After a year, we had to transfer to a permanent school. I chose Colgate University, and Dick picked Cornell. We were accepted, graduated in 1950, and went out into the world again.

My first job after college was as a salesman for Borden Milk Co. selling glue. It was a job that taught me how to sell—the hard way—door to door canvassing, but they cut back and let three of us new men go. Then I found a home at Keuffel & Esser Co. From salesman, I went up the line to branch manager, director of training, and finally national director of sales. However, the company was bought out too many times, and it finally disappeared.

The greatest event in K&E was meeting my future wife, Carol. She was reassigned as my assistant and eventually became my dear wife. Little did she know that we would be moving around the country for K&E. In St. Louis, our daughter, Cathie, was born and two years later, in Los Angeles, our son, Jim, was born.

Now Cathie works in the corporate section of a super market chain as Consumer Affairs Coordinator. Her second marriage is to her former high school classmate Vincent Miller, and they are a blended family with five children: Allegra, Vito (VJ), Brandon, Ryan, and Justin.

Our son, Jim, retired after 30 years working for the Morristown NJ Police Department, and is now an active duty Commander in the U.S. Coast Guard in Virginia. He is married to his greatest supporter, Kat, who works as a physical therapist in the Navy Hospital in Portsmouth VA.

Long marriages seem to run in my family. My brother, Martin, celebrated more than fifty years. My brother, Bill, and I both exceeded the fifty-year mark.

Most recently, it has been fun researching and learning about the details of my Army past. Those French and Belgian towns still remember us, and many celebrate every year—the day of their respective liberations back in 1944-45.

It is also good to know that I wasn't alone in my ignorance of many of the details, such as exact locations or names of battles, the exact organization of our regiment, etc.

The thing I did know was that the men beside me would do whatever necessary to move forward to stop the enemy.

Almost sixty years later, I watched the newscasts about that fateful flight, United Airlines Flight 93 on September 11, 2001. It was so similar to the attack on American soil December 7, 1941. It was also to be remembered thereafter only by the date it occurred, and I realized the truth of what it means to be an American. When circumstances are at their most dire, strangers will band together for the good of our country—and the people that they love.

EPILOGUE

James K. Cullen II

When I arrived in Afghanistan I found myself in charge of my own team of military members, and was assigned my own armored vehicle. Half-tracks had been retired years before; I received an up-armored Series 998 HMMWV, or "Humvee". I thought about my father's experiences in WWII and the men he lost there, and so I named my armored vehicle "ELEANOR II". I wrote the name on the HMMWV's dashboard where I would see it at all times. That served as both a homage to my Pop and the men he served with, and also as a constant reminder to me to do my best to be a good leader and look out for my people.

In the 1990s, D.O.D. had been in touch with a re-enactors' group out of Washington state who had modeled themselves after dad's Third Armored Division unit. In a tribute to my father and his men who fell in battle, they had crafted uniforms and vehicles that carried the same insignias and markings as Pop's men in Normandy and the Ardennes. The re-enactors invited my dad out to see them and give talks and ride along during a mock "battle", and it was very humbling. They had painted one of their half-tracks with the markings of E-12 "ELEANOR", and it was very moving for him to see.

(James K. Cullen with replica WWII half-track, E-12, "Eleanor")

(James K. Cullen center with WWII reenactors Chuck Anderson left and Steve Borts right.)

For my father's 90th birthday, my family made a tribute video with various family members sending contributions from around the country. I did some research and discovered that the re-created ELEANOR from Washington had been purchased by a collector in Connecticut. I was able to eventually reach the new owner, Art Dias, and he was very supportive. He invited me to come there to see the half-track and make a video. On his birthday I was able to surprise D.O.D. with a video of me in my military uniform, driving ELEANOR out of the woods and wishing him a happy day.

(Replica Half-track)

Later that year my wife Kathy and I told my mother that we had a surprise for Pop, and we were taking him on a short trip to see an old friend. We picked him up in New Jersey and went on a road trip to Hartford, CT, where he was reunited with ELEANOR. He got to climb up into the Troop Commander's seat of "E-12", right where he rode when heading into combat in the 1940s, next to an engraved plaque naming all the men who served with

"Eleanor". He was wearing his old Third Armored Division uniform jacket. I had the honor of driving D.O.D.'s old armored vehicle in the Veterans Day parade, with spectators cheering my dad as he rode in the same position on the vehicle as during World War II. I'd be lying if I said I wasn't choked up.

In 2013 the military officially designated ELEANOR II the HMMWV a historic artifact, and she was shipped back intact to the USA from Afghanistan. She is now on display in New Jersey at the NAS Wildwood Museum at Cape May Airport, while her permanent home is built at the Coast Guard Museum in New London, CT. She is publicly displayed with a plaque that references my D.O.D.'s service and the sacrifices of the brave men who served with the original ELEANOR in World War II.

ELEANOR E-12 the halftrack continues to appear at parades and car shows in the northeast, still carrying a plaque with the names of the men who served on the original vehicle. Hopefully she will remain a living tribute to my father and his men who fought in the hedgerows of Normandy and the frozen woods and villages during the Battle of the Bulge.

PART II

Seventy Years Later

Editor's note: The following is a collection of the author's thoughts and observations on the military since his retirement as a civilian businessman. It is related to, but not an extension of, the story of Band Of Strangers. Rather than chapters, there are headings to indicate the major theme of each section.

I believe there is great value in Mr. Cullen's thoughts and perspectives of our country's last seventy-three years. I hope all readers will take the time to read this section and learn from it. As the twentieth century scholar, George Santayana wrote, "Those who cannot remember the past are condemned to repeat it."

The search for facts:

In 1997 Stephen Ambrose wrote *Citizen Soldier*. That and other books and films started to revive interest in World War II. *The Good War* by Studs Terkel, *The Longest Day*, and *Saving Private Ryan* showed the public that the GI had done an enormous job in defeating the Germans and Japanese. Interest in what we did back in 1943, 1944, and 1945 became strong.

"Where on earth was I?" was the question I began asking myself, in the years after I retired from Keuffel & Esser Co. I read the 3rd Armored Division history book, *The Division*, published in Germany, which was sent to all of us who had been in the outfit. I tried to relocate myself in the many actions described in the book, and some of the names and places were slightly familiar, but not all. I needed more information—and accurate information.

For example, I knew that I had been in Task Force "Lovelady" in Trois Ponts, in 1944. The Division history, though, said that it was "B" Co. of the 36th with Lovelady in the Order of Battle. I was confused—was I in Trois Ponts or not? And if not, where was I?

On a visit to Belgium in 1984, I borrowed a car and drove to the Ardennes to visit the village. Everything was just as I remembered. The twin viaducts, the houses, the hills, and the river; I had definitely been there! When I returned to the States I re-read the book, and then it hit me. Col. Lovelady always worked with the 2nd Battalion, never the 1st Battalion. We in E Co. were 2nd Battalion.. B Co. was 1st Battalion. I wrote letters to the Division Historian and eventually got an answer. He and Col. Lovelady agreed with me; the book was wrong. E Co. and I *were* in Trois Ponts in 1944.

After that, I started to read WWII history books, trying to make sense of our wild trip across France and Belgium and into Germany. The books, though, all concentrated on the Big Picture and the broad brush. I sought closer detail.

There is a Military History Institute in Carlisle, Pennsylvania. I heard that they had collections of material from all U.S. Army units. They did have books, papers, photographs, and personal histories from all the divisions and separate units. Also, they cataloged the official army histories of the campaigns and battles. There were several copy machines available, and I reproduced many pages that were written about my division and its battles.

Then I learned that "After-Action Reports" were retained in the Archives in Washington, D.C. These papers were usually written shortly after a battle and seemed to be what I wanted. One of the workers at Carlisle gave me a letter of introduction, and the address in Suitland, Maryland.

I went there within a few weeks and started a long and interesting series of visits to the Archives. Each time I went there, I learned more and more about the actions and activities of my division and regiment, but nothing about the platoon level.

Reunions and others like me:
In 1990, I learned of the 3rd Armored Division

Association, so I joined and went to a few reunions. Out of the hundreds of members at those reunions, I knew only one person, "Chief" Alejandro. There were other men from E Co., but I didn't know them. Some had joined after I left the division, or they might have been in another platoon or squad.

Then I found the Veterans of the Battle of the Bulge and joined that organization. It has a great group of men, all of whom were in the Ardennes in 1944. A monthly meeting at Picatinny Arsenal in New Jersey brings the group together for lunch and a talk on some military matter. They are a fine bunch of old soldiers.

A commentary on modern views of history and battle:

Many of the Veterans of the Battle of the Bulge, or VBOB for short, give talks about WWII to a variety of groups including high school students. The young students get very little study work on WWII, and we just give them a glimpse of what went on during the war years. They ask many good questions, and hopefully they realize what their grandfathers went through back then to ensure the freedom they enjoy today.

At one school I asked to see a textbook, and the teacher gave us the pages on WWII that he had copied. We found only two sentences on the Battle of the Bulge. Here is all that was written:

"The Germans attacked the American lines on December 16, 1944. The lines of the U.S. Divisions were bent, but did not break, and they recovered to defeat the enemy."

All I, and thousands more had been through—freezing nights, lost men, terror, and triumph—reduced to two sentences in a textbook.

Our school visits were an attempt to teach the students. When we visited the high schools in the early 2000s, some students usually asked us, "What did you think of *Saving Private Ryan*?

That usually started a good discussion about

Hollywood films. Hollywood has made a great many films with a war theme over the past sixty years. I haven't seen all of them, but I have seen a few. Not many of them were very good. By "good" I mean realistic and true to what I had seen in action.

I remember one Hollywood film called *A Walk in the Sun*. It took place in Italy. Some GIs were in a ditch when they looked up to see German planes high overhead. The Sergeant shouts, "They're Nazis. Douse that (cigarette) butt, soldier."

What a laugh! Some films had infantrymen in the field in immaculate uniforms with clean shaves. That didn't happen in the ETO.

The Story of GI Joe—Ernie Pyle's film biography, was a very fine movie. All the scenes and the soldiers appeared to be the real thing. The story follows Ernie Pyle as he travels throughout the Italian Campaign with different Infantry units. The one sequence on Captain Walker is special. It is very emotional and captures the feelings of an Infantry Company when their CO gets killed.

Another good one was *Battleground* a story about "The Bulge." It didn't strike a wrong note throughout the whole film. The acting was great, and the uniforms and the gear were very accurate. The story was about Bastogne, but that was OK. The outfits on the Northern Shoulder of the battle didn't think that Bastogne deserved the publicity it received.

The film follows one squad as it fights through the Bulge. There is a lot of humor in the movie, and that is true of action in war. It isn't all grey and gloom—there were a few laughs.

Now, to answer the question about *Saving Private Ryan*. In my personal opinion, that movie is a bad one. There was detailed accuracy on the uniforms and gear, and the opening cemetery scene and the closing one, were hard to take. They were very emotional and close to home. In between, though, the actions and tactics of the GIs were unbelievably bad. The captain makes a frontal assault on a German machine gun post—up a hill—in daylight and gets two of his men killed. His mission was ignored for the sake, I guess, of action in the movie.

Then in the village fight, they attack a Kraut tank with sticky bombs (a grenade inside a stocking then coated with grease to make it "stick" to a tank's hull.) This trick was rumored to have been tried in Italy, but it sounds like wishful thinking, based on my experience.

Hollywood isn't totally at fault in the making of war films. They simply can't duplicate the confusion, the panic, the boredom, or the smell of real combat. But sometimes they do come close, as in *Battleground*.

Overseas alliances and research:

I started to look further afield, and I found CRIBA, (Centre de Recherches et d'Informations sur la Bataille des Ardennes, or Center of Research and Information on the Battle of the Bulge), a Belgian non-profit group that does research on the Bulge and publishes action reports on the Internet.

In the 3rd Armored Division Association newsletter, I saw the name Henri Rogister several times and knew that he was an official at CRIBA in Belgium. I had a photo of a Belgian village that I had clipped from the US Army magazine, *Yank*. It was an aerial shot of the village, deep in snow, taken during the Bulge. I sent a copy to Mr. Rogister asking if he could identify the town. It looked very familiar to me. I thought that it might be a town we had taken.

He shot back an answer immediately—the town was Regné and the 3rd Armored had attacked and recaptured this town in January. With his letter he also sent photos of the present-day village, and how it had recovered from our counterattack. At last, I was learning where I had fought.

We exchanged many letters after that. He asked me for eyewitness accounts of actions I had been in, and he gave me answers to my many questions. I told him about the house we were billeted in, in Trois-Ponts, and Henri identified the old woman we had seen who was shot by the SS. Henri also knew the names of each of the nineteen Belgian civilians shot that day by the Germans.

I asked him about the civilian we had shot in another town in Belgium, the one with the papers with swastikas. Our people had spotted him as a sniper. Henri passed my letter to Anne-Marie Noel-Simon and her husband, Karl. The only identifying landmarks I could recall were the church and the alley across from the church. Anne-Marie traveled the roads of Belgium tracing our division route, looking for the church and the alley. She sent me photos and maps of many villages, but nothing I recognized.

Then, I remembered the picture I had taken of S/Sgt. Stan Rich when he was lying on the sidewalk in front of the alley. I also remembered Stan had been a policeman before he was drafted. We called him "Flatfoot." I asked my son, Jim, then serving as a Lieutenant with a police department in New Jersey, to try to trace Stan.

Stan had lived in Seattle. Jim contacted the Seattle police and obtained the address of Stan's widow. Stan had died some years ago.

I wrote to her, and she sent me the photographs that I had taken over sixty years before. I sent copies to Anne-Marie, and she matched the photos to a spot in Eupen, Belgium. Anne-Marie sent me newspaper accounts and eyewitness stories about that little action. A German rear guard unit had set up an anti-tank gun to try to stop us. An officer with a pistol was directing the Krauts when Stan and his squad surprised them. The officer shot at Stan and hit him in the legs. The Germans then ran; our men didn't see them, and insisted they saw the poor postman. The Belgians said, at the time, that the anti-tank guns fired at our tanks when we changed our route, but I doubt it. I'm sure it was another anti-tank gun way down the road.

I have had a very good relationship with my Belgian friends. During my visits to the National Archives, I have been able to obtain information to help them in their research on the Ardennes campaign.

Back to the headgerows:

One day a few years ago, I was idly searching 3rd Armored Division information online and found a site for a re-enactor's group in the Pacific Northwest. Searching further, I found that they had taken the 36th Armored Infantry as their "unit" to replicate. I contacted the Webmaster, Steve Borst, and told him that I had been in the 36th. That started one of the most enjoyable episodes of my life.

We e-mailed back and forth as the men of the group asked me questions, and I tried to answer. They knew more than I did about our gear and equipment, but I had used it in real action and could answer from that perspective.

I am still amazed at what I didn't know then but have since learned. For example, I thought that E Co. 1st Platoon consisted of three Rifle Squads, and that was it— at least that's all I ever saw. I was shocked to later learn that we had a Mortar and a Machine Gun Squad. They were the 4th and 5th squads in our platoon. I learned this at a reunion in 2003. Where were those people when we needed them in action? I guess that illustrates how narrow our focus was.

The enemy was also a great unknown to us. We knew that we faced German soldiers, but we didn't know really if they were SS troops or Panzergrenadiers, or just plain German troops, or even Volkssturm, or what. Not that it really mattered. They were the enemy who wore a gray uniform and that's all we needed to know at the time.

Years later I learned that the enemy we faced were the 2nd SS Panzers at Mortain, and the 1st SS at Trois Ponts.

Regimental Distinctive Insignia are the little badges GIs wear on their lapels to show that they belong to a particular regiment. I didn't know the 36th Armored Infantry had a badge until I saw one at Carlisle Barracks,

PA in 1998. I've since acquired several of them and put two of them on my old uniform "Ike" jacket where they belong.

The re-enactors group invited me to come to the West Coast to participate in an "event"—to me it was called a sham battle. I said, "No thanks," but then they sent me a note saying that they would pay my expenses for the trip. After thinking about it for a while, I decided to go, and had a most wonderful time.

For the "battle", they gave me a full uniform and choice of weapons. I chose a nice, light .45 in a holster. I was shocked at how much an M1 rifle seems to me now! In 1944, the M1 was like part of my right arm.

With other re-enactor groups, we participated in an "event." We attacked a German bunker at Ft. Stevens State Park, Oregon. I rode in a jeep and felt like a general going off to war. There was a lot of blank ammo fired, and everyone had a fighting-good time. As usual, the American side won.

The squad and I had dinner and I thanked them for adopting my Company E as their unit. They had restored an old half-track and painted it with my track number and name, E-12, Eleanor. They gave me a ride in E-12, and it was a very emotional experience.

We correspond regularly by e-mail, and I consider those men out there very close friends. After my trip to meet them, I wrote a letter to say they made me feel like I was back with my old squad in 1944, explaining to them that when I left my squad on a hill above Cherain, I thought that I would never see them again. But these re-enactors made me feel as if I were home again with my group back in 1944. It stirred up memories of the men who had made it through the Bulge, and those who had lost their lives in the battle.

It was a warm and memorable experience never to be forgotten.

Seeing the bigger picture:

I'm proud of my service with the 3rd Armored Division. I didn't choose it; the Army made the choice for me. Thinking back, I am happy the Army placed me where they did; to me and to many historians, it was the finest fighting unit in the U.S. First Army.

In trying to learn more about the history of the 3rd Armored and the battles it fought, I read a great deal about WWII. I learned about Kasserine Pass in North Africa, Anzio and Salerno in Italy, and Iwo Jima and Guadalcanal in the Pacific.

In the European campaigns, I read about Bastogne, Mortain, Mons and Trois Ponts. I found books about the famous generals, complete histories of the war, and books about individual battles and campaigns. Those that I didn't buy, I picked up at the library. I tried to read them all.

Eventually, I read about battles that happened thousands of years ago. The author and historian, Victor Davis Hanson, took me through the Peloponnesian Wars and the Greek and Trojan Wars. I learned that men through the centuries fought their battles at arms' length with swords and spears until the English longbow taught them to kill at a distance. I learned about Linear Warfare, the way kings and princes lined up their armed men in precise rows on a chosen battlefield, then ordered them forward to fight, while they—the kings and princes, sat on a nearby hill and watched.

The American Indians taught the British and American Revolutionary soldiers to fight using cover and concealment. But eventually, both sides still lined up in ranks to fight. Not until our war in 1941 did we fully apply the lesson.

The machine gun and rifle made the lesson stick. No soldier could stand still on an open field and live very long. We *had* to keep moving, and use cover and concealment.

The tactics and technology of war always change. Our Civil War introduced trench warfare and ironclad battleships, and WWI saw the extended use, and demise, of both of those fighting methods. The airplane and the aircraft carrier, for all intents and purposes, a mobile airfield, for example, killed the battleship.

Thoughts on leadership:
The WWII generals all wrote books or had volumes written about their strategies and war plans. Eisenhower, Bradley, Patton, and Montgomery were all on the shelves. But the only one that dwelt on my part of the war was *Lightning Joe Collins* written by General Lawton J. Collins himself.

As Commander of the 7th Corps in the First Army, General Collins was the General Officer who had direct contact with our Commanding General, Lt. Gen. Maurice Rose.

General Collins had fought in the Pacific and then had been called to our fight in Europe. From reading his autobiography and other histories, I learned that Gen. Collins was a thoughtful, intelligent gentleman. He directed the divisions under his command with a firm hand and used constant pressure to move us forward. I learned that he didn't like the way our Commanding General, Leroy Watson, was performing in Normandy. Watson was relieved, and Gen. Rose was brought in from the 2nd Armored Division.

Major General Maurice Rose (1899-1945), the son of a rabbi, was the leader of the 3rd Armored Division from Normandy to Germany. He led our troops with cold, hard precision, and in my opinion, was a tactical expert far superior to any of the other commanding generals.

He plotted the historic attack of the 3rd Armored Division in the one hundred twenty-five-mile encirclement of 350,000 Germans in the Ruhr Pocket. At the head of the attack, he was killed in action when he was shot by a young German tank commander.

Major General Rose was the only U.S. General to be

killed in the ETO in action.

General Collins was also a "pusher." That meant he gave his subordinates their orders, and then pushed them to meet their objectives. Col. Lovelady was also a pusher. They all were!

None of us wanted to run toward the enemy and face his fire, but when we were pushed, we did it. Of course, most of the time we didn't need pushing; we knew what we had to do. On all the fronts in WWII, the GI managed to figure out how to defeat the enemy, regardless of the odds. All of our planes and artillery did not win a foot of ground. The only one who did that was the GI with his rifle; all the others helped!

During our war in France, Belgium, and Germany, I knew what life was like in the foxholes. As part of the sharp edge of our First Army, I dug my way across Europe. To learn what life was like in the upper echelons, as I said previously, I read a number of books on our Generals—Eisenhower, Bradley, Collins, Montgomery, and our own Gen. Rose. All had their biographies and memoirs.

But the one with the most ink was Gen. George Patton. This man was idolized by most of the war correspondents, and they wrote story after story about him and his outrageous talk. They loved him because he was always good for a headline. Not all correspondents liked him though. Ernie Pyle despised him and never mentioned his name. Bill Mauldin, the cartoonist and writer, also disliked him and his methods and drew pictures poking fun at Patton and his Third Army discipline and policies.

In the 3rd Armored Div. we learned to frown when we heard Patton's name for two reasons. The first had to do with the shortage of gas as we approached Germany. We heard that some of Patton's 3rd Army troops had stolen gasoline from our petrol dump at gunpoint, and when Patton learned about this caper, he laughed his head off. The other event was a series of errors in the newspapers.

War reporters would send back a report that "the 3rd Arm'd" had taken a town. The editors changed the 3rd Arm'd to 3rd <u>Army</u> and gave the credit to Patton! To this day, people hear "3rd Armored" and think "Patton's Third Army."

Ever since the War, historians and writers have constantly given undue credit to this pompous, egotistical blowhard. For example, during the Bulge, the town of Bastogne was by-passed by the Germans on their mission to get to the Meuse River bridges. After the town was surrounded, Patton's 4th Armored Div. broke through the German line to relieve the town and ever since, Patton has been given credit for winning the whole Ardennes Campaign. Utter, utter nonsense!

The historical facts are these:

The German 6th Army, led by Joachan Peiper, was charged with the mission of penetrating the Allied Forces and to capture Antwerp on the Belgian Coast. All this action was in the North of the Belgian area, with the 82 Airborne, the 30 Infantry Division, and the 3rd Armored Division concentrated in the Trois Ponte area and committed to stopping the German thrust. The three divisions did just that by destroying Pieper's forces.

In the South at the village of Bastogne, the German column initially by-passed the village and ignored the U.S. Troops that had been rushed to this area. Then Hitler, for some reason, demanded the capture of the village. The German forces encircled the area and thereby neutralized the 101 Airborne and the 10 Armored Division. They put up a great defensive fight, but defensive action does not win a war.

The American press painted an heroic picture of Patton racing to the rescue of the American Divisions, and then concluded that the "Bulge" was erased by Patton's very expensive cost in G.I. lives and gave all the glory to him, and that picture is still the press's idea of what happened in the Ardennes.

Regarding the Bulge, the American Press knows only three words—Bulge, Bastogne, and Patton. Well, it's not true and historically speaking—this is all "Nuts".

The war in the air and the Pacific Theater of Operations"

The Pacific War, where my brother Martin fought was in one aspect, different from the ETO. The armies in the ETO went into a fight on foot or on the back of a tank. In the Pacific, the soldier and marine were carried to the fight by the U.S. Navy and delivered to the beach by the U.S. Coast Guard. The armies of the ETO fought to deny the ground to the Germans, while the forces in the Pacific fought to take away and occupy an island so it could be used as an airbase. We attacked Germany on a broad front, while the men in the Pacific approached the Japanese homeland on an island-to-island tactic.

Air power was a big factor in the final destruction of the enemy's homeland. In the ETO the Air Force bombed the cities, factories, and transportation while we, the soldiers, went after the German army on the ground. This combination destroyed Germany.

Japan, on the other hand, was pounded for months by our Army and Naval Air Forces with the final blow winning the war—atomic bombs dropped on Hiroshima and Nagasaki.

The army since 1945:

In 1950, I watched Korean War from a distance. I saw from the pictures that the soldiers were wearing the 1944 gear and using the same weapons. The only big changes were the recoilless rifles and the jet fighters.

Like the Bulge, the fighting in Korea was a dogfaces' war. There was no good tank country—it was all mountain and rice paddies. The GI had to take the high ground all by himself—with help from the air and artillery—to stay alive.

Our army was pushed around quite a bit during that war, or Police Action, as it was called, and didn't really win in the end. We drove the enemy, Korean and Chinese, back to the 38° Parallel where it all started, and that is where it ended. But we still have thousands of GIs stationed at the line today. Korea turned into a political mess when Gen. McArthur's ego got in the way of his military thinking, and it ended in a stalemate.

My wife's young cousin, George Baker, was killed in Vietnam. He was in the army and volunteered to lead a patrol into the jungle. That was his last mission.

His death made the war more personal, and I watched this fight closely. The GI (now called a Grunt) had automatic weapons, and he could throw more lead in five minutes than my entire squad could in half an hour. But again, the jungles were bad tank country, and this time the GI rode into the fight in the cabin of a helicopter. These little birds were introduced in Korea and found their place in "'Nam."

These vehicles inserted the troops into a fight, left them, and then came back later to pick them up again. The helicopters did the transporting of the ground troops to and from the combat area. When they "extracted" a company from the jungle, they flew them back to an established encampment with all the comforts of the rear area. The men enjoyed good food, movies, radios, beer, and showers for a short period, then they were taken back to the combat area to fight again.

I don't see how this could be good for a soldier. Being in combat week after week, as we were in WWII, was not good for a man's nerves, either. However, it was better to stay at the job and get it done, rather than being dropped into battle for a short time, then extracted to sit in the rear echelon camp and *think* about going back into the fight. Sometimes the imagined fight is worse than the real thing. A soldier's objectives in Viet Nam, from what I can tell, were to kill some enemy and then come home. Our objectives were to kill the Krauts, occupy the territory, and win the war. By denying him ground, he had to run to new territory with us after him.

In Vietnam, the battles were designed to add up enemy dead, not to actually take the enemy territory. There was no strategy to actually win the war. The few pitched battles that were fought, though, were won by U.S. troops every single time.

Another factor in Vietnam was the rotation system. Soldiers served a tour and at the end of the tour, they went home. The Tour of Duty in the Army was twelve months. Our WWII service was "for the duration": continuous until the end of hostilities, or you were wounded or killed. I'm sure that in Vietnam, a GI's mental state and fighting ability must have been affected as he approached the end of his tour. Who wanted to be killed the day before he got to go home?

Once again, politics ended the fight, and the American newspapers and newscasters like Walter Cronkite, soured the nation on the whole affair. The media, not the enemy, defeated our Army.

Vietnam was a bad fight because the Air Force mistakenly thought they could win the war with bombs alone. Bombing a target without the infantry occupying and taking that target is a waste of time, bombs, and lives.

The "Cold War" went on during this period, starting with Sir Winston Churchill's speech at Missouri calling attention to the "Iron Curtain" which had descended on Europe.

In some places the "war" was pretty hot. Russian pilots flew MiGs over Vietnam, our submarines played "chicken" with Russian subs, and men like Steve Borts in the 3rd Armored Div. faced the huge Russian Army in Germany and denied them any expansion into Europe. This was a period where the whole world wondered if the nuclear bombs would go off again.

Vietnam ended and so did a lot of poor practices in the Army. The draft was stopped, and an all-volunteer force took its place. We watched the Army clean out the "ticket punchers" and the dead wood. A new spirit grew in the service, and all of us veterans watched it grow with pride. Our Army was looking like the one we left in 1948. It was a winning, aggressive, ready-for-combat force.

The War on Terror is still ongoing. It is a fight against Islamic extremists who want to take the world back to the 12th Century. They don't wear uniforms nor have formations and ranks. They just have munitions that they hide as booby traps and do their killing from a distance—a really nasty war.

According to the Division history of the sixteen armored divisions in the European Theatre of Operations, the 3rd Armored Division saw the most combat, inflicted the most damage, and took the most casualties. The 3rd Armored Division was deactivated in 1992. The flags, standards and battle streamers were cased; they are probably in Ft. Knox or the new Army museum at Ft. Belvoir.

More than sixty years later, a message sent to Colonel Lovelady sums up the spirit of American soldiers and civilians over the ages, when faced with terrible odds.

When we crossed the German border (in WWII), General Collins sent congratulations to Col. Lovelady, "Tell Lovelady he's famous. Now tell him to keep going."

He and his band of strangers did.

ABOUT THE AUTHOR

James K. Cullen, the son of Scottish Immigrant parents, tried to enlist in the armed services at the age of seventeen, just after the bombing of Pear Harbor on December 7, 1941. He was turned down because he was still considered a British subject but was eventually drafted by the U.S. Army, by which he earned his citizenship. He was a drill instructor at Ft. McClellan in AL for a year and a half, then volunteered for a transfer to the front.

He served in the European Theater of Operations from 1943-1945 and participated in some of the most significant battles of World War Two. He was awarded four Battle Stars, a Bronze Star, a Purple Heart with Oak Leaf Cluster, Combat Infantry Badge, and Belgian fourragere of 1940. After release form the army at the end of the war, Jim took advantage of the opportunity offered by the G.I. Bill and graduated from Colgate University in 1950.

After retiring from a successful civilian career as a businessman, he became involved in numerous veterans' organizations, including The Battle of the Bulge Group and World War Two Reenactors in the U.S. northwest. His friends in these groups encouraged him to write about his experiences. Band OF Strangers is the result of many years spent researching the facts and recalling his own experiences as a young, 21-year-old Army Staff Seargant.

Jim is still married to his beautiful wife, Carol, after more than fifty years. He has two married children and five grandchildren.

Name: James K. Cullen
Born: Scotland 1923
Education: BA Colgate University 1950
Occupation: National Sales Manager, Keuffel & Esser Co.
Status: Married with two children
U.S. Citizen U.S. Army 1943 Rank S/Sgt.

Ft. McClellan, AL—Drill Sergeant
Joined 3rd Armored Div., 36th Armored Infantry on
Normandy.
Wounded September 13 in Germany
Wounded January 18 in Belgium

Awarded four battle stars—Normandy, Northern
France, Ardennes, and Germany
Bronze Star
Purple Heart with Oak Leaf Cluster
Combat Infantry Badge
Belgian fourragère of 1940
French Legion of Honor 2018

James K. Cullen II is a Commander with the United States Coast Guard in Hampton Roads, VA. A 9/11/2001 first responder, he spent seven years of his career working with the U.S. Army and Joint Chiefs of Staff supporting Operations Iraqi Freedom and Enduring Freedom – Afghanistan. He currently serves in the command cadre of U.S. Navy Coastal Riverine Group Two at Joint Expeditionary Base Little Creek. He retired honorably from a career as a New Jersey police supervisor, served as Chief of Police for the U.S. Coast Guard Police in New York City, and is now with the Portsmouth, VA Sheriff's Office. He holds a Juris Doctor degree from Rutgers Law School and currently attends post-graduate studies at the Naval War College.

Made in the USA
Columbia, SC
01 December 2021

50168438R00140